...בכל לבבך...

...With All Your Heart...

WITH ALL YOUR HEART

Insights into the Inner World of
Israeli Hero Major Roi Klein

Based on discourses by Rav Eliezer Kashtiel
Edited by Netanel Elyashiv
Translated from Hebrew by Sharon Blass
Cover designed by Ben Gasner
Interior designed by "Two Designers" studio

Machon Binyan HaTorah
14 Ha'Alon st. Eli, Israel 44828
(972) 994-4141
www.binyanhatorah.com   info@binyanhatorah.com

ISBN 978-9-65740-713-4
Printed in Israel by Old City Press

With All Your Heart...

*And you shall love Hashem your G-d, **with all your heart**, with all your soul, and with all your might.*

(Deut. 6:5)

With all your heart *– with both of your inclinations, with the inclination to good and the inclination to evil.*

(Talmud Bavli, Brachot 54a)

With all your heart *– That you should be wholehearted in your devotion to Hashem.*

(Rashi on Deut. 6:5)

***With all your heart**, I interpret to mean: with all of the powers of your heart, that is, all of the powers of the body, because everything begins from the heart, and the import is: that you must make the object of all of your endeavors – to know G-d.*

(Rambam, Guide to the Perplexed, Book I, chap. 39)

Roi Klein

2 AV 5735 (1975) - 1 AV 5766 (2006)

Table of Contents

Preface

At a time of longing and pain, it is hard to write, but ultimately, the feeling of gratitude prevailed.

First of all, my thanks to Shoshana and Aharon, parents of Roi. Thank you for cultivating a diamond in your home, for providing the house where this wonderful son of our Holy Land flourished. Thank you for agreeing to turn us, his friends, into part of the family, part of the memory. Thank you for your courage in being constantly involved in discussing Roi's character, with all of the pain entailed by opening a still-bleeding wound. Thank you for making your house a regular meeting place for Torah where we studied together every month, and where – thanks to your generous cordiality – the group was able to coalesce and together absorb the teachings of our Rabbis. The tranquility and humor, the openness and candor that prevail in your home are undoubtedly what created the conditions for all of us to come together and study subject matter relating to a precious individual who is no longer with us.

My thanks to the members of the family who accompanied the classes with their presence, expressing interest and involvement. Thank you for the great nobility, which you manifested by your desire to attend a class about a person whom you knew and loved. Certainly great modesty is required to listen to a talk about a brother and husband given by someone who is a not a member of the family.

My thanks to the group of friends, who came regularly, thus enabling a continuity of study, a serious-minded atmosphere, and a gradual development of ideas. A special thanks to the Davidovitz and Elyashiv families for organizing the class and making sure that it continued to meet.

My thanks to Rav Netanel. Were it not for his diligence, this book would not have been published. Thank you for your keenness, your painstaking thoroughness, and your enlightening comments and additions, as well as the pleasure that I had from every conversation with you.

Wistful yearnings for a beloved person are hard, and we have tried to alleviate them with words of Torah.

Memories of a beloved person are painful, and we have tried to find consolation in aspirations to improve and reform.

The vacuum is great and we are trying to fill some of it by learning about what we have lost, and what we must make up.

When the righteous depart this life, their image arises and a flame bursts out, and gleanings, sparks that are gradually collected, shed a faint light on our lives which have been darkened, which have been dimmed, with the passing of the righteous.

Eliezer Kashtiel
Menachem-Av 5767
One year without Roi

Foreword by the Editor

The story of Major Roi Klein, a hero of the nation of Israel, who in the Second Lebanon War gave his life in sanctification of G-d's name, has yet to be told in the detail it merits. This book in his memory, released (in Hebrew) on the first anniversary of his fall in battle, serves a different purpose. It consists of lectures given during the year of mourning at the Klein Family home in Ra'anana to Roi's family and friends by Rav Eliezer Kashtiel, head of the 'Bnei David' Kollel in Eli, Israel.

From the time of his arrival at the military-preparatory yeshiva program 'Bnei David' in Eli, Roi was constantly deepening his connection to Torah, both during his active military service as well as during the leaves he was given between assignments. His most productive period of development came in his last years when he was sent by the IDF to complete academic studies. Roi chose to earn his degree at the College of Judea and Samaria in Ariel located near Eli, so that he would be able to devote as much time as possible to studying Torah in the yeshiva in Eli. For nearly three and a half years, while also starting his own family and completing a degree in Industrial Engineering and Management in addition to the other projects assigned to him by the IDF, Roi devoted the best part of his time and energy to Torah study, and the quality of his identification with its sanctity advanced steadily: day after day, semester after semester, and year by year. His study session would begin at five thirty in the morning and usually continued until late afternoon. By dint of hard work and perseverance, he covered many of the difficult topics in Torah study: many chapters in the Talmud tractates of Kiddushin, Nida, Yevamot, Ketubot, and Menahot, all studied in depth with the classic commentaries; a large section of Hoshen Mishpat in the Shulhan Aruch, books by the Maharal of Prague and Rav Kook, the Netziv's commentary on the Torah ('Haamek Davar'), and more. A large part of this learning was done with his study partner Rav Eliezer Kashtiel. This is the source of his deep familiarity with Roi, which is reflected in the lectures you have before you.

Each lecture deals with a quality that characterized Roi. At times, sections of Roi's notes taken from the notebooks he left after him are integrated into the lectures. It should be emphasized that Roi wrote these notes as he studied and were never intended for publication. We have decided nonetheless to bring them as they are, with only minimal revision, when needed for editorial purposes or out of technical difficulties.

Roi's name was mentioned explicitly in these lectures on only a few occasions, and generally at the end of the lecture, but those who knew him, knew that, in fact, the entire lesson was about him.

"When I call on the name of Hashem, ascribe greatness to our G-d". Roi ended his life in this world calling out the name of Hashem, and we are obligated to continue that call, giving greatness to our G-d, among other ways, by learning from Roi's qualities.

May it be Hashem's will that these words serve to exalt still further the soul of our beloved friend Roi, whose soul was exalted while it was still among us in this world to such lofty and awe-inspiring heights.

Netanel Binyamin Elyashiv,
Machon Binyan HaTorah,
1 Menahem-Av 5767
One year after the death of Roi in battle

Foreword to English Edition

The Jewish nation has always strived to emulate the great heroes and the nearly superhuman spiritual giants with which it has been abundantly blessed. For many generations, our role models were to be found, by and large, in our written and oral Torah. This admiration of our heroic predecessors and of our national and spiritual forefathers was expressed in the famous words of our sages:

> *Each and every one of the people of Israel must ask himself: when will my good deeds reach those of my forefathers, Abraham, Isaac, and Jacob.[1]*

The miraculous reawakening of our nation which led to the establishment of the State of Israel has given the modern day Jew still another, relevant, more immediate, though far less spiritually exalted source of inspiration: that of the leaders and fighters of the Zionist movement, the State of Israel, and the IDF.

For too long, it seemed as if these two sources of example and inspiration contradicted each other: if you were moved by the life-story and teachings of Rabbi Akiva, of the Rambam or of the Vilna Gaon, you were unlikely to feel for the likes of Herzl, Jabotinsky or Moshe Dayan, not even for their dedication and courage in helping establish a Jewish state; and if you did feel for the latter, you probably wouldn't be at ease with Torah-oriented role models. If you were lucky enough to identify with the vitality and majesty of the inner light of our life – the Torah – and at the same time also with the national valor and strength embodied in the heroes of Zionism and the State of Israel (if not with some of the other, less admirable aspects of their behavior), you were likely to feel some degree of dissonance or conflict, an inner contradiction.

But what appears to be an unbridgeable gap is actually nothing more than an illusion. The standard, facile distinction made

---

1   Eliyahu Rabba, parasha 23.

between what is labeled by many as "Judaism" as opposed to what is referred to as "being Israeli", vanishes once we recognize the shared source of both what is "Jewish", and the good, pure part of what is "Israeli". Knesset Yisrael – the Jewish nation as an ideal, a timeless reality with a special link to Hashem that expresses itself throughout history in the Jews of every generation – is indeed the hidden, inner wellspring that nourishes our Judaism as well as our national life.

This belief – which was in short supply as we took our first steps in the long process of our national revival, and which was the core of the philosophic-spiritual system of the Torah giant: Rabbi Abraham Isaac Hakohen Kook – is spreading. More and more Jews understand the natural relation between these two integral components: religion and modern nationhood. In the past few years, we have witnessed the emergence of refined, sensitive souls, men of great stature, who identify with the whole, truly indivisible stature of the Jewish nation.

This book is a living memory of one of these special people, Major Roi Klein hy"d. Roi perfectly combined in his personality the "Jewish" traits with the "Israeli" ones, both in his noble life and in his heroic death.

In his life, a combat officer who studied the *daf yomi* – a substantial daily portion of Talmud study; an excellent student of industrial engineering and management who began his secular studies only in the afternoon, enabling him to delve into the deep sea of Torah study from the early hours of the morning until late in the day.

In his death, the officer who redefined bravery and courage in Israel's Second Lebanon War, as he leaped on a live hand grenade to save the lives of others while sacrificing his own, who clearly and loudly said *Shma Yisrael* with his last breaths.

Our nation has paid too heavy a price because of the imaginary contradiction between what is deemed "Jewish" and what is deemed "Israeli". It is time for reconciliation. This was Roi's deep belief; he lived for it, and also, to our utmost sorrow, died for it.

Since Roi's death sanctifiying Hashem's name, his story touched the hearts of Jews throughout the world. We therefore thought that translating the book, thus enabling the large English-speaking Jewish community to read it and be uplifted by it, is well worth the effort. Our hope is that Roi's noble personality, which is elucidated in these pages, will reach out and touch Jews worldwide, helping them unveil the noble Jewish traits and deep connection to Israel within their own souls.

Finally, I wish to thank the people who have helped make this edition possible: Sharon Blass, for taking on the lofty job not only of translating Rav Kashtiel's discourses, but also of dealing with the challenging task of translating the esoteric, profound writings of the great Jewish luminaries – the Maharal and Rav Kook. Rabbi Jonathan Blass, for his wise counsel and enlightening comments. The talented Ben Gasner, for designing 'With All Your Heart' with all of **his** heart. Above all, my dear wife Noa, for being there during the whole process, with everlasting patience and sound advice.

Netanel Binyamin Elyashiv,
Machon 'Binyan HaTorah',
Eli, Israel.

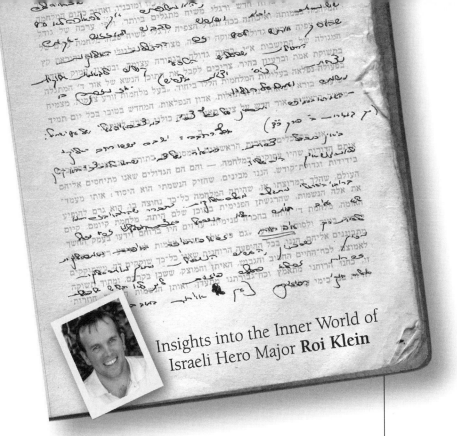

Insights into the Inner World of
Israeli Hero Major **Roi Klein**

Chapter 1

As soft as a reed: The quality of *Adinut*

As soft as a reed: The quality of *Adinut*

A. As delicate as a *tola'at*

B. Adinut as the goal of development

C. King David's refinement of soul

D. The primary source of adinut: Torah

E. A second source of adinut

F. The third source of adinut: constant teshuva

G. The refinement and sensitivity of Roi

A. As delicate as a tola'at (worm*)

Our rabbis comment on the meaning of the names of King David's warriors and interpret each name to symbolize one of David's personal characteristics. In explaining one of these names – 'Adino Ha'etzni'[1] – the rabbis explain that the name expresses David's ability to contain within himself seemingly conflicting characteristics:

> *When he sat and engaged in Torah study – he made himself as delicate as a tola'at, and when he went out to do battle – he made himself as firm as a tree [etz, as in the name 'Ha'etzni'].[2]*

The expression 'made himself as delicate as a *tola'at*' is a curious one. David himself uses the word '*tola'at*' in the Book of Psalms in describing himself: "But I am a *tola'at* and no man"[3]. The *tola'at* is a creature without a shell, without a thick skin, and therefore it symbolizes the quality of delicacy, of refinement, whose opposite

---

1   **II Sam**. 23:8.

2   Tractate *Moed Katan* 16b. See also **L'emunat Itenu**, IV, 123.

3   **Psalms** 22:7.

* The term in Hebrew does not contain the negative connotations of the English word 'worm'.

qualities are toughness and inflexibility. The Talmud in the
tractate *Ta'anit* says:

> *A person should always strive to be as soft as a reed
> and not as hard as a cedar, and that is why the reed
> was chosen to produce the quill used to write the Torah
> scroll, tefillin, and mezuzot.*[4]

Why, then, is hardness one of the qualities comprising the soul of
man? This is apparently a defense mechanism that man uses when
he discovers that reality can sometimes be menacing or frightening.
There are aspects of reality that do not suit us, things that are very
different from the way we are, and because we feel threatened, they
cause us to feel great emotional stress. In response to a perceived
threat, man encases himself in a covering – a shell – of toughness
and rigidity allowing him to coexist with a complex reality, one
that is difficult and turbulent, one that he cannot always flow with
smoothly and seamlessly.

As part of the attempt to place this quality of *adinut* – delicacy
or refinement – at the center of our spiritual world, we shall try to
study several essential paths toward building a new consciousness
that can be the basis for living a life where this quality of *adinut*
may grow and flourish. We shall also try to clarify for ourselves
the importance of *adinut* by focusing our inquiry on King David.
It is especially interesting to see how the soul of this warrior and
military general, of all men, demonstrated *adinut* so prominently
in his character even when he was facing harsh and complicated
predicaments.

---

4   Tractate *Ta'anit* 20b.

B. Adinut as the goal of development

First it is important to establish the development of the quality of *adinut* as a main purpose in life, not as an afterthought, "icing on the cake", but as a primary goal one must strive for.

In *'Orot Hateshuva'*[5], Rav Kook ranks the refinement of soul as a central, universal objective of a society and of culture:

> **Integrity born of spiritual purity dictates every endeavor of knowledge should be directed toward the constitutive ideal of shaping the human will in accordance with the greatest purity that befits it, to refine the will, to strengthen it, sanctify it, purify it, to condition it through various educational exercises so that it always aspires to what is noble and exalted.**

When man is honest, when he is true to his Godly nature, to the Godly reality that he has within him, he strives toward refinement of his soul, *adinut*. All of human development and growth is a kind of cleansing aimed at that supreme goal, of refining human will. All pursuit of technological and industrial development must also be directed toward helping man develop within himself a more refined humanity, to create a life that requires less roughness and sparring, a life where it is simpler to be gentle and refined toward ourselves and toward our environment.

> **Let the sciences deal with the issue of how to realize in the physical world all of the individual instances of good which are the goals of the beneficent and honest wills that determine the character of the world. It is these particulars which constitute all of life's proper material and spiritual requirements. But the ultimate purpose of the sciences must be the refinement of the**

---

5   **Orot Hateshuva** 15, B.

will itself, its intellectual clarity and the expression of the will that is at its essence.

Because we have within ourselves wills characterized by spiritual purity, science and knowledge in general have an important role, namely, to serve these wills. Human knowledge can greatly enhance our ability to help the sick, for example, or to travel quickly from one place to another for important purposes; but the infrastructure, the wellspring that motivates the entire world of knowledge must be the **will for good.** Ultimately, after all progress and development, we must reach the main goal, "the" subject: man, his will, and the level of its refinement, the measure of his ability to live a life that is not one of fierce competition, as though he were perpetually living on a battle field.

In this context, it is proper to mention another source, a letter Rav Kook wrote to the editor of one of the newspapers of his time clarifying the role of the educational system.[6] In the letter he explains that we – the Jewish people – are accustomed to the idea that the world is not a jungle and that our main objective in life is not to train to succeed on the battlefield of life but rather to build a different personality; it is not a world of conflict, where our main aspiration is to triumph over our fellowman and to be the strongest. He explains that since the days of our forefather Avraham we have been trying to educate toward something different, toward shaping a person who is honest and good. Therefore we have to moderate roughness wherever possible and to increase refinement and gentleness. Since this is the chief objective, resources must be invested in shaping this inner refinement, in devoting thought to the question of what is the social and ideological basis for refinement of the soul, towards building a society whose lifestyle is the refinement of the soul. This may not be prevalent in our society, and yet there are people living among us who can serve as examples and role models, who maintain

---

6   **Igrot Ha-Reiyah**, I, 218-219 [no. 170].

a very rich and active lifestyle while their behavior is very refined and gentle, without roughness and belligerence. As we have already seen in the words of the rabbis, it is specifically the thin, flexible reed that was chosen to be associated with the most elevated of objects, the Torah, tefillin, and mezuza.

Rav Kook goes on to say in Orot Hateshuva:

> **But woe to humanity when it deviates from the straight way, and instead of establishing the center of all its progress on the basis of ennoblement of the will – it leaves the will in its coarse state without developing and uplifting it, and all of its endeavors are only to fulfill the will's desires which flow like a river of sulfur, controlled by all kinds of emptiness and evil.**

Here is a severe admonition against a world where science and technology develop rapidly, while the purification and refinement of spirit do not keep pace. In such a reality, the end-product of all progress will be merely the gratification of our material desires. And in such a world, science and technology might, G-d forbid, actually bring down destruction upon the world.[7] That is why the center of all human development must first and foremost be a heightened refinement of the soul.

C. King David's refinement of soul

Before we explore ways to build up the quality of *adinut*, as a theory and as practical instruction, let us contemplate one example taken from the personality of King David, whose character was also described as: 'Adino H'aetzni'. The situation portrayed is highly stressful, when all around him everything is going up in flames, and

---

7   See elaboration in **Kodesh ve-Hol**, pp. 111-132.

one might expect rougher, and less forgiving conduct; however, at that point David chooses to express rather his gentleness and refinement of spirit.

Our story takes place in the period preceding David's rule, when he was living, together with his followers, in a small place called 'Ziklag'. At a certain point David and his group, six hundred men, leave the town in order to investigate the possibility of joining a battle campaign. After several days they return and find their place burnt to the ground and desolate of life. They soon discover that a band of Amalekites had swooped down on the town and carried the women and children off into captivity. The men return to find the town nothing but scorched earth, and as the text states: "**They raised their voices and wept, until they had no more strength to weep**". Their grief was so great that it caused them to turn against their leader David, even to the point of wanting to stone him! David, through Evyatar the Kohen, asks Hashem what to do and the answer that he receives through the Kohen's mediation, using the *Urim ve'tumim* (within the Kohen's breastplate; a means of ascertaining Hashem's will through a form of prophecy) is that he should pursue the Amalekite force that devastated the town.

The text reads[8]:

> *So David went, he and the six hundred men who were with him.*

Let us try to put ourselves into that situation: David takes 600 men, all fearful and anxious. Their wives and children have been taken captive by the Amalekites, and these men are about to set out on a dangerous campaign to rescue them. David advances quickly and reaches the brook Besor, while fully one third of his troops are unable to maintain the pace:

---

8   **I Sam** 30.

> *David pursued, he together with four hundred men,*
> *while two hundred men remained, who were too*
> *exhausted to cross the Besor brook.*

Since those who remained behind were also warriors, it is clear that the pace has been grueling in hot pursuit of the Amalekite troops. David advances with his remaining forces when suddenly:

> *They found an Egyptian man in the field and took him*
> *to David; they gave him bread and he ate, and they*
> *gave him water to drink.*

As though it were not sufficient that David's men fed him bread and water, the text states that they also gave him "a piece of a cake of figs, and two clusters of raisins", in our terminology: 'sweets'.

> *And when he had eaten, his spirit returned to him, for*
> *he had not eaten bread nor drunk for three days and*
> *three nights.*

Why had this Egyptian , abandoned by the Amalekite army, gone so long without food, almost to the point of death?

> *David said to him, "To whom do you belong? And*
> *where are you from?" He replied, "I am an Egyptian*
> *youth, the slave of an Amalekite man. My master*
> *abandoned me because I became ill, three days ago.*

His Amalekite master was a cruel person, emblematic of the national character of Amalek, and when he saw that his servant had fallen ill, he made a simple financial calculation. It did not pay to keep on a sick servant and so he left him behind, to die in the desert. But the youth, apparently unaware of the identity of the people he had just met, spoke candidly of what had just transpired, undoubtedly shocking David and his men:

> *We raided the South of the Cherethite and the territory*
> *of Judah and the South of Caleb, and we burned down*
> *Ziklag with fire.*

Excellent, this is the man we are seeking! He was an accomplice to the burning of Ziklag! It is logical that they do not execute him summarily since he is valuable to them as a source of intelligence, useful only if he is left alive to reveal the whereabouts of the troops. However, we do expect a vigorous demand that he hand over the information immediately; we even anticipate the use of threats and intimidation. But that is not David's style. With all of the need and desire for quick results, he is facing an enfeebled, exhausted individual, and he addresses him with great gentleness:

> *So David asked him, "Will you lead me to that band?"*

And the youth, instead of being grateful that he has not been killed on the spot, has the temerity to lay down conditions:

> *And he replied, "Swear to me by G-d that you will not kill me nor hand me over to my master, and I will lead you to that band."*

Apparently the youth did not require much time to assess the character of King David, for he seemed to be more apprehensive of a reunion with his Amalekite master than of any immediate danger to himself, ostensibly posed to him by David. If that is the case, then both from the text itself and from the nature of the youth's response, we understand that David treated him with great gentleness.

The text goes on to describe how this same gentle, refined man stormed the Amalekite troop, launching a successful surprise assault, during which he and his men killed that entire criminal band down to the last man, except for four hundred young men who managed to escape on camels[9]:

---

9   Editor's note: Since the verse states that they killed everyone except for four hundred young men, one may infer that the troop was very large, consisting of at least thousands of warriors; in this light, David's achievement is intensified, in his having defeated the troop with only four hundred men. The numerical inferiority of the rescue force turns the complaint of the four hundred men against their two

> *And David smote them from twilight until the evening*
> *of the next day; not a man of them survived, except*
> *for four hundred youths who were riding camels, who*
> *fled.*

One can only imagine the astonished expression on the face of the stunned Egyptian youth who suddenly realizes that the man he considered a "bleeding-heart" pushover has shown himself to be a fierce warrior and a military hero...

We encounter both of these sides in David's personality for which he earns the nickname 'Adino haetzni': delicacy and patience towards the Egyptian youth in a situation where, frenzied and tense as it was, there was no real need for violence, together with a terrible ferocity towards the enemy when that was required.

The continuation of the story only serves to heighten the evidence of David's delicacy:

> *So David rescued everything that Amalek had taken,*
> *and David rescued his two wives. No one among them*
> *was missing, from small to great, sons and daughters,*
> *as well as the spoils, including everything they had*
> *taken for themselves; David returned everything.*

This prodigious achievement lifts morale, and the angry feelings towards David give way to a sense of admiration and veneration.

> *David took all the [Amalekite] sheep and cattle; they*
> *led them before that livestock and said, "This is the*
> *booty of David."*

However, it still had to be decided how to divide "David's spoil". This decision depended on what the people's attitude would be

---

hundred comrades who stayed behind with the baggage (as described below) into more understandable, and intensifies the nobility of David's response as well, since he bears them no grudge.

to the two hundred warriors who had lagged behind, and hence lacked the glory of the brave warriors who were victorious on the battle field:

> *David then came to the two hundred men who were too exhausted to go follow after David, whom he had stationed at the Besor brook, and they went to meet David and to meet the people who were with him. David approached the people and inquired after their welfare.*

First of all, David takes the initiative in addressing them in a friendly way, his greeting to them stemming from a desire to appease them and give them a good feeling, a sense of belonging even though they had not managed to participate in the fighting. However, among David's men are a band of men who are disturbed by this sensitive, noble attitude; they want the spoils to remain only with those who actually fought:

> *Every mean-spirited and base person of the men who had gone with David spoke up and said, "Since they did not go with me, we will not give them of the spoils that we rescued, except to each man his wife and his children; let them take them and go."*

David clearly does not share the competitive-triumphant attitude of this group, and he tries to teach them a lesson; but here, too, he takes pains to do this with the utmost delicacy:

> *But David said, "Do not act so, my brothers, with that which G-d has given us, for He has watched over us and delivered into our hands the band that had come upon us. Who could hearken to you to such a thing! Rather, like the portion of the one who remained with the baggage; they shall divide it equally."*

David's method is consistent; he is not reproachful but rather uplifting.[10] The aggressive people who are referred to in the text as 'base fellows', he calls 'my brethren' and emphasizes that what is at stake is not 'David's spoil' but G-d's spoil. He institutes a law to be upheld for all times among the people of Israel whereby those who go out to battle shall be treated like those must remain behind not by choice but for lack of ability to fight.

Thus, throughout this turbulent event, David is revealed as a highly refined personality toward the Egyptian youth, toward the warriors who stayed behind, and in his gentle rebuke of those people who demanded that those who remained behind be deprived of their share.

D. The primary source of adinut: Torah

It is, however, not enough to characterize the quality of *adinut* as a goal; we must ask ourselves how can we develop this quality within ourselves. Studying the writings of Rav Kook reveals three fundamental sources which have the power to give rise to the quality of adinut, which we so yearn to achieve.

The first source relies on the grammatical root of the Hebrew word *adinut* – the letters ayin, dalet, nun – (ע.ד.ן). which in Hebrew is associated with *eden*, or the garden of Eden. We are used to saying Garden of Eden as a single, undivided phrase, but if we read the Torah verses precisely, we will see that it is not written that way: **"And the LORD G-d planted a garden eastward, in Eden"**[11]; and **"And a river went out of Eden to water the garden**[12]. Eden, then, is not the garden but the source: There is water there from which a river flows to water the garden where **"every tree that is**

10 See at length in **L'emunat Itenu**, II, 21-40 [Hayashar k'David].
11 **Gen.** 2:8.
12 Op. cit, 2:10.

pleasant to the sight, and good for food"[13] grows. It would then appear that 'Eden' is a source spring, a root, a place of bubbling or gushing, where streams emanate and enable growth. Therefore, throughout the Tanach, 'Eden' is an expression for source. That is what Sarah says when she is informed that she will give birth at the age of ninety: "**After I am waxed old, shall I have rejuvenation [in Hebrew: *'edna'*]**"[14] – I am returning to a state of *eden*, the original state, to my root. The objective that lies behind our desire to return to Eden is the desire to belong to the point of the wellspring, the place where one can receive a new issuing forth.

Adinut, or refinement, is connected to *eden*, the source. The ability to be refined is related to the question of what is the wellspring that causes our thoughts and the stream of our lives to flourish. A person can live a life where all that directs and guides him is what is happening outside of himself, in his environment; when he sees something interesting, he is attracted to it and when he sees something threatening, he is wary of it. A person like this may perhaps be situated in the garden, but he is lacking the wellspring. He is living in the world but his reactions are determined by the events that take place around him. One must know that it is possible to live a different kind of life, a life that is connected to some Eden, a life where we are always striving to fill ourselves with content, with influence and spiritual streams that come from a lofty and deep-rooted source. A life lived this way is inevitably a refined life. It is not dependent on its surroundings, for the person who lives such a life has an inner source of life which he draws upon. This source is the Torah. The Torah is Eden, and it is called 'the tree of life'[15], because by virtue of it, we create an independent life, a life that is suited to our inner being, that is not dependent on what is happening outside of us.

---

13 Op.cit. 2:9.

14 Op. cit. 18:12.

15 **Prov.** 3:18.and in the **Metzudat David** ad. loc. "For those who grasp it, it is a tree of life for them, because one can attain life through it."

And thus Rav Kook writes in his book 'Orot Hakodesh'[16]:

The highest thoughts of holiness (kedusha), that emanate from the source of the holy (kodesh), from the light of Torah and of wisdom (ḥochma), refine people's souls and add to them the light of true life.

There are elevated thoughts that are not taken from the world surrounding us but from a different source, and they generate desires and aspirations beyond what is derived only from "what is happening on the ground". These thoughts contain an aspect of Eden; they come from a transcendent source. These are the inner thoughts of the Torah. When a person accustoms himself, slowly but surely, to creating a wellspring from which he elicits worldviews, aspirations, and moral guidelines, a wellspring that constitutes a replacement for the habitual, superficial sources that most people draw their impressions from – his soul becomes increasingly refined. A person like this is not dismayed by the fact that reality around him is different. He learns to observe the world around him with patience, because he knows that in the end, the higher impressions that he lives by will ultimately work their uplifting influence on the entire world.[17]

One should pay particular attention to the emphasis in the words of Rav Kook: These thoughts add to the soul the light of **true life.** This life is true because it is loyal to itself; it does not change continually in accordance with the vicissitudes of a changing reality, nor is it threatened by these fluctuations, and thus this life has no need to cope with the world in a rough way. A person who makes himself as delicate as a *tola'at* when he is engaged in Torah study and tries with all of his might to absorb the meaning of the Torah into his inner being – is a person who wants this content – this and no other – to have a maximum

---

16 **Orot Hakodesh**, II, 295 ["Eden hakedusha"].
17 Based on the continuation of that passage of Rav Kook.

presence in his innermost soul. This kind of connection with the Torah progressively refines his character.

We were privileged to observe this process in Roi's consistent development. His personality demonstrated clearly how his effort and perseverance affected the delicacy of his soul, his thoughts, and desires, his ways of coping with various challenges – the overall flow of his life.

The more a person associates himself with exalted thoughts – and this association is not measured so much by the quantity of time devoted to them as it is measured by his spiritual connection to them – so, too, his position facing Eden enables him to draw more and more from the river that goes out of Eden.

A number of books mention this allusion: the initial letters of the words *eden*, *nahar*, and *gan* [eden, river, and garden, respectively] form the root word ע.נ.ג(oneg = delight). We are commanded to call the Shabbat' a delight[18'], and based on what we have learned, this means that the Shabbat is a declaration of the existence of life that is different that what most people are presently living, a higher level of life, more connected to our source, a life of sanctity. On the weekday we are driven by all sorts of exigencies, first and foremost the need to earn a livelihood, but on Shabbat, all external constraints are eliminated, and we are free to allow life to be propelled by a different motive, to draw upon another source of inspiration. The life flow drawn from the world of the holy (*kodesh*), from a day that is completely Shabbat*, is called a 'delight'; on Shabbat we encounter the river that goes out of Eden, and we take delight in a source that comes from G-d. There is a close connection between the degree to which we accustom ourselves to live a life which revolves around *adinut* and the spiritual quality of the Shabbat that we experience. A person who lives a very delicate life anticipates the coming of

---

18 **Isa.** 58:13.

Shabbat because that is the time that *adinut* can be fully expressed, much more than on the weekday. On Shabbat there is less of a need for harshness, wrangling, and toughness. We do not want to escape reality using the Shabbat, but we do want to deepen our connection to the wellspring, using its power to approach reality on the weekday in a more refined way. It is on this day that we spend more time involved in contemplation of sanctity, of Torah, and these thoughts are the key source for creating delicacy in life.

E. A second source of Adinut

In another volume of *Orot Hakodesh*, Rav Kook sheds light on another source from which we may draw *adinut* into our lives:

> **It is the anticipation of salvation that purifies the soul, increases knowledge, and refines the spirit.[19]**

How can anticipation of salvation refine the spirit? In order to understand this, we must make sense of the term 'anticipating the salvation.' On the surface it seems that anticipating salvation is a passive quality. If that were the case, there would be no reason to expect that passive waiting would make a person gentler and more delicate. However, anticipating salvation is in fact a very dynamic activity, to the point where the Talmud states that one of the questions a person is asked on the day of judgment is : Did you look forward to salvation?[20] The first question he is asked is if he had scheduled regular times for studying Torah, which is the first point discussed here. Afterwards he is asked if he looked forward to salvation – did he possess the certainty, the firm faith, the resolution of soul, prayer, and entreaty that salvation would indeed come. Why is it so important to believe that the salvation

---

19 **Orot Hateshuva**, III, 353 ["Tzipiat he-yeshua"].
20 **Talmud Bavli**, *Shabbat* 31a.
* a reference to the world to come

will come? Why has faith in the coming of the Mashiach been established as one of the 13 articles of our faith[21]? How is this faith capable of causing *adinut* to grow within us? Perhaps the answer to these questions entails the understanding that the person who is anticipating salvation is filled with confidence that the good ultimately will prevail, and even when current reality is rough, complex, and harsh – the world will ultimately be fully good and pure, refined and sanctified, a world in which "the wolf shall dwell with the lamb"[22]. A person who is confident in the triumph of good – is filled with the recognition that this is the right order of things, that refinement serves a purpose. If the world is now in the throes of a process that will eventually lead to life that is refined and holy, it is a sign that it is right to shape our lives in this spirit even now! Refinement is not "being spacey" or ignoring reality; on the contrary, it is a way of orienting ourselves toward the reality that will ultimately take over the world. The faith that humanity will eventually work its way up to the level of a truly moral life gives strength and hope, encouraging us to be better already now.

The more a person is filled with the anticipation of salvation, the more optimistic he is, and he is not readily disappointed by the fact that reality has not yet reached its highest level. He is optimistic not because it is a more pleasant way to live, but because it is clear to him that reality is not a wasteland, and the King of the Universe will ultimately cause it to be filled with the good that derives from G-d. This belief develops in us a great deal of **patience;** man learns that he will not lose anything by choosing to live a refined life; on the contrary, this is how he can live in harmony with the real laws of the universe, which are at present hidden from our view. We are

---

21 "And the twelfth principle is – the coming of the Messiah, which is to believe that he will come and that he will come at the appointed time... and to believe in his greatness and that one should love him and offer prayer for his coming, as spoken of by every prophet from Moshe to Malachi. And anyone who casts doubt on him or who makes light of his word – is speaking falsely of the Torah." **Hakdamot Ha-Rambam** (Rav Y. Shilat ed.), p. 145 [Introduction to 'Helek'].

22 **Isa**. 11:6.

secure in our faith that this law-like order will emerge buoyant out of the depths and fill the world as historical fact. We do not live reality only according to its present manifestation, rather, we know where it derives from and where it is headed, "With joy shall you draw water out of the wells of salvation"[23], from the wells of the exalted future from which we draw the principles by which we will build our lives in the present.[24]

F. The third source of adinut: constant *teshuva*

The third root from which we can draw the strength to develop *adinut* in our souls appears in Rav Kook's work **Orot Hateshuva** [25]:

> **Making the idea of teshuva* a permanent part of one's thought is what establishes the character of a person on a basis of nobility, and he then constantly absorbs into his inner being a delicate spirit.**

The thought of *teshuva* stems from a belief that man has the ability to change himself, the ability to tell himself: "While it is true that yesterday I was like that, today I can be different".[26] The thought of *teshuva* is a thought that comes from freedom and dynamism. This freedom, this power of man to make significant changes in his life is an expression of delicate refinement, because when a

---

23 **Isa.** 12:3.

24 For more on anticipating salvation, see **Tzadik B'emunato Yichye, pp.** 143-144; **Kodesh ve-Hol, pp.** 73-75.

25 **Orot Hateshuva** 9,1.

26 "How great is the power of teshuva, that it brings man closer to the Divine Presence...Teshuva brings closer those who are far. Yesterday this person was hateful in the eyes of G-d, loathsome, removed, an abomination, and today he is beloved, delightful, close, a friend...How great is the merit of teshuva, yesterday he was alienated from the G-d of Israel...and today he is attached to the divine presence..." / **Maimonides**, Laws of Penitence, 7: 6-7.

* Teshuva as defined by Rav Kook means repentance as part of the return of man (and with him, all of creation), to an increasingly greater connection with his Divine source).

person is harsh to his environment and harsh to himself, when he is dogmatic, closed and impervious, he is unable to make any real changes in his personality. He generally does not even believe that change is possible. A person who is capable of opening himself to change, who knows how to forgive himself and to begin anew is a refined and sensitive person, and it is likely that this *adinut* will also be demonstrated in his attitude to those around him. Just as he believes in his own power to change, so will he believe in his fellowman and will not rush to declare that the flaws in people are irredeemable. By virtue of this belief he will know that it is right to treat his fellowman gently even when the latter behaves in a way that would seemingly justify his acting harshly and severely.

The world of *teshuva* is closely connected to the quality of mercy (*rahamim*). A superficial observation might equate mercy with unjustified leniency and over-indulgence; in actuality the quality of mercy is associated with the quality of truth because it stems from the rightful realization that man is truly capable of changing himself for the better. To be as soft as a reed means to temper the quality of justice with the quality of *hesed* [giving when it is not required or deserved]; the advantage of the reed is that it can be extremely flexible without breaking. Thus the quality of justice becomes more flexible until it appears as the quality of mercy. However, this flexibility is not a breakdown of the quality of justice, so that "whoever who says that G-d has renounced the exercising of justice – shall have his own life renounced".[27] The habit of thinking constantly about *teshuva* builds, then, a personality which has much capacity for gentleness and flexibility.

---

27 **Talmud Bavli**, *Bava Kama* 50a. Rashi explains: "renounced" - abandoned. To see the reconciliation of the contradiction between the quality of mercy and the quality of justice, see the Ramhal in **Mesillat Yesharim**, end of chapter 4.

G. The refinement and sensitivity of Roi

If we return to the noble, refined character of King David, we will discover that he excelled in precisely these three fundamentals: David dedicated so much of his time to Torah study to the point where the Talmud says that he almost never slept, so ardent was he to arise and to engage in Torah.[28] The longest chapter in the entire Tanach is chapter 119 of the Book of Tehillim (Psalms) which is in its entirety a song of praise of love of the Torah and the desire to uphold and observe it. There is also no greater symbol of anticipated salvation than King David: our prayer for salvation is identified with King David personally: "The offspring of Your servant David may You speedily cause to flourish". In addition there is no one comparable to David as a person who did penance, so much so that the Talmud says of him that "he established a yoke of teshuva".[29] David sinned but he also knew how to repent. He believed with perfect faith that he was capable of repairing what he had damaged; he pleaded to be deserving of the ability to do *teshuva*, as one can readily see in his wonderful songs of teshuva among the chapters of Tehillim.

In summation, when I examine the last six years during which I knew Roi and we studied together, there is no doubt that one of the major things that could and should be learned from him was the aspiration to heighten the quality of *adinut* and to place it at the center of our lives, at the center of our social and educational aspirations. I remember that when we studied tractate *Yevamot*

---

28 **Talmud Bavli**, *Brachot* 3b.
29 **Talmud Bavli**, *Moed Katan* 16b; *Avoda Zara* 5a.

together, I told him – parenthetically to a discussion on the
issue of converts – that I had accompanied a couple during their
process of preparing for conversion, a process whose high point
was when they stood before the rabbinical court to be accepted
as Jews. I described the moving occasion which they had looked
forward to so much and prepared for – where they replied to the
questions of the rabbinical judges, until the head of the court told
them to stand up and declare that they believe in the G-d of Israel,
and the written Torah and the Oral Law, and they uttered these
words as an expression of the greatest truth of their lives. It was
only after Roi was killed that I heard from Sara that he had gone
home that night and shared with her my story of the converts. He
was so sensitive that as he told the story, his eyes welled up with
tears. He did not know these people, but it was enough for a man
of his sensibilities to hear about the occasion of their entry into
the faith of Israel to move him to tears. That is only one small
example. *Adinut* lay at the center of his life, and it deepened, by
virtue of his constantly being influenced by the three sources of
adinut we have discussed: the Torah, anticipation of salvation,
and constant thoughts about *teshuva*.

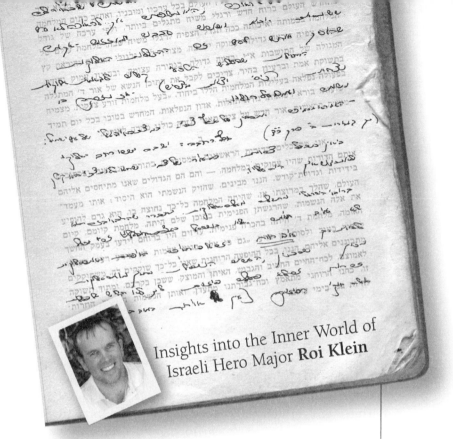

Insights into the Inner World of
Israeli Hero Major **Roi Klein**

Chapter 2

Spiritual Thirst

Spiritual Thirst

A. Let the heart of those who seek G-d rejoice

B. And from the wilderness – a gift

C. Fire and Water

D. Thirsts Coming Together

E. Thirst for knowledge of G-d

F. Roi's thirst for knowledge and life

A. Let the heart of those who seek G-d rejoice

In this lecture we will try to illuminate another aspect of Roi's character. One of his most conspicuous qualities, one that I learned much from, was his spiritual thirst. Spiritual thirst is what leads a person to be diligent, to search, and to progress. Let us try to investigate the subject of spiritual thirst.

The prophet Amos says:

> *Behold, days are coming, says the L-rd G-d, that I will send a famine in the land, not a hunger for bread, nor a thirst for water, but for hearing the words of the LORD.*[1]

It is true that this prophecy spoke of impending divine punishment, but it also contains a positive note; it describes a period when we will feel an increased desire for spiritual improvement: to know more, to learn more, to set as our aspiration, as an end in itself, constant spiritual progress.

In the morning prayers we recite the verse: "Let the heart of those who seek Hashem rejoice" [Psalms 105:3]. A person must achieve the level where he is considered 'one who seeks G-d', to be

---

1   **Amos** 8:11.

continually in a state of motion, of searching and progressing, and by dint of these, he will possess perpetual enthusiasm and vibrancy, a special motivation that is defined in the Psalms as 'joy'.

In his commentary on the prayer book '*Olat Reiyah*', Rav Kook explains this verse:

> **We come to the realization that the inner longing of seeking G-d is greater than any other expression of life and of happiness, and that the search itself is the attribute that is sought and not the finding of that which we are seeking, which is always unattainable. For we are striding forward from greatness to greatness, from quest to quest, from clarity to clarity, and from certainty to an ever higher certainty.**

This explanation represents a revolution in the conventional terminology: we learn that man can reach the greatest happiness not by focusing in on a finite objective and achieving it but rather by being a constant **seeker**. With great things that can never be fully attained, seeking is more important than achieving, the effort is more important than the finding. The way to reach them is to seek them unendingly, to move up from one level to the next, to go from one achievement to the next.[2]

B. And from the wilderness to Mattana

In his book '*Tiferet Yisrael*' which deals with the revelation at Sinai and the giving of the Torah, the Maharal (Rabbi Yehudah Loew of Prague, 1512-1609) devotes an entire chapter to the fact that the Torah was given deliberately in the desert, as it is written in the verse: "And from the wilderness to Mattana"[3]. – mattana, in addition to

---

2   See, among others, Rav Kook's **Ein Ayah**, *Brachot*, chap. 4, par. 43.
3   **Numbers** 21:18.

being a place-name, is also the word for 'gift' – the gift, which is known as the Torah, was given, of all places, in the desert. This might seem to be a marginal piece of information, even slightly bizarre: Couldn't a more conventional place be found to give the Torah? Also the *midrash* highlights the basic idea of the Torah being given specifically in the desert[4]. In the text itself the 'headline' beginning the chapter dealing with the giving of the Torah is: "In the third month after the children of Israel were gone forth out of the land of Egypt, the same day they came into the wilderness of Sinai"[5].

The Maharal explains in the chapter dealing with this subject that the desert is not only the description of a locale; in the context here, it is primarily **not** a locale but a spiritual-attitude of man. There is a kind of person who feels that he is already settled in life, that he has "built" himself, and he has clear-cut definitions for every subject; he feels that he has reached a certain fullness in his life, whether in his understanding of the world or in his expectations of himself, in his spiritual makeup. A person like this can be compared to a built city, a settled and orderly place. It is very possible that he has many fine qualities – but thirst is no longer one of them. He is not in an emotional position that demands curiosity, and his eyes are not the eyes of innocent earnestness that reflect a desire to know more, because he is already satisfied with himself. By giving the Torah in the wilderness, it is as though Hashem is saying to us that in order to derive the maximum from the Torah, we ourselves must be in a "wilderness" state of mind. We do not have to be physically in a desert locale, rather it is sufficient to be open to new ideas, to new feelings, and to emotional changes. This is a state of the soul that is reminiscent of a field that has never been plowed, a landscape untouched and unmarked by the human hand, and in the words of the Maharal, it is being "outside of the settled area".

---

4   **Bamidbar Raba**, A.
5   **Ex**. 19:1.

The perspective of the soul which originates in a place of questioning and expectation is very characteristic of the Book of Psalms. King David spent a considerable amount of time in the wilderness, under less than fortuitous circumstances, usually as a hunted fugitive. However, he was able to use that situation to derive spiritual benefit. In the Book of Psalms, there are many descriptions that are related to both thirst and to the desert landscape. It is the extent of the thirst that later determines how great is the satisfaction at slaking that thirst, the extent of the fulfillment and joy over what a person has succeeded in learning.

The emphasis on the fact that the Torah was given specifically in the wilderness teaches us a general principle: it is beneficial when a sense of wilderness and of spiritual thirst precedes the study of Torah. Thirst is necessary as an attitude that allows a person to open up to new vistas, to fresh development. This thirst also frequently brings with it a sense of enthusiasm, which is characteristic of a person who looks forward to something that he has not yet attained.

C. Fire and water

The *midrash* states: "The Torah is compared to three things: wilderness, fire, and water"[6]. Along with the wilderness discussed above, two contrasts appear in the *midrash*: fire and water. The thirst produced by the wilderness breeds two qualities which seem to be opposites: fire and water. In '*Orot Hakodesh*'[7] Rav Kook writes about thirst as a spiritual experience, and fire and water both appear as different stages of this thirst:

The great flame of thirst for knowledge, of yearning

6   **Yalkut Shimoni**, Parashat Yitro, par. 246.
7   **Orot Hakodesh**, III, 212 [s.v. "Shalhevet tza'ar va'eden"].

for righteousness, agitates the life-force of those who
are pure of spirit...

The flame that burns in the heart of man, the yearning that he has
within him to live a life that is more honest and truer, is fiercer
particularly among those who are pure in spirit, who have an
honest earnestness;

It propels them to compelling and unending labor. They
will know no tranquility or rest, they will be mad with
transcendent love and compelling passion...

This turbulent, existential thirst that is found among the pure of
spirit gives them no respite; they are compelled to very great efforts
because of their love and passion. This is very appropriate to the
words of the rabbis who wrote that "Torah scholars have no rest,
neither in this world nor in the world to come"[8]. One must not
misunderstand the nature of this thirst: it is not an expression of a
mental affliction or a disorder of any kind, on the contrary: it is a
most desirable quality.

And in their hearts they are always sorry and trembling,
yet they are filled with assurance and courage, abundant
hope, an awe born of their nobility, a generous eye, a
depth of penetration, a sensitivity to flaws together with a
willingness to rise above all sin.

In these Torah scholars there is the aspect of perpetual unease caused
by the fact that they have still not accomplished all that they should
have. However, their anxiety is not an anxiety of the incapacitating
type but rather a noble anxiety that comes from their constantly
asking themselves: Have I done enough to slake the thirst burning
in me? They are characterized by possessing a generous, discerning,
and inquiring view of things, and are therefore prepared to seek what
will quench their thirst in every possible place.

---

8   **Talmud Bavli**, *Brachot* 64a; *Moed Katan* 29a.

The flame of love and unbounded giving (*hessed*) rises with the height of its waves, and its fire – a holy fire – burns with great fierceness

Until now Rav Kook has been describing thirst using the metaphors related to fire; from here on he shifts to using metaphors related to water. In his writing he describes the quenching of this burning thirst using the image of learning, spiritual progress, and personal improvement:

With the waters of the Torah, of wisdom and of knowledge, with the waters of prayer, of teshuva and of closeness to G-d, of righteousness, of generosity and of charity, in which, in its magnificent desire, the virtuous will is immersed, the edge of the burning, flaming thirst is quenched and a settled, quiet spirit begins to reveal itself, only to reignite again and to act as a life-force of grand and lofty proportion.

The spiritual thirst is somewhat satisfied. There is a sense of peace and tranquility, the satisfaction that comes from a genuine spiritual achievement that has been attained, evocative of a person who slakes his thirst with pure, cold water "as cold water to a thirsty soul"[9].

D. Thirsts come together

In a passage following the one previously quoted, Rav Kook deals with various types of spiritual thirst[10]:

It is important to distinguish between the particular types of thirst for knowledge of G-d .

---

9   **Prov.** 25:25.
10 **Orot Hakodesh**, III, 313 [s.v. "Hitmazgut hatzimonot hakedoshim"].

> Sometimes what waxes strong is the thirst for
> Divine enlightenment directly from the source, an
> enlightenment that flows from the neshama (soul) by
> virtue of the neshama's attachment to the Divine truth
> and from the power of the neshama's purity.
>
> And sometimes what waxes strong is the thirst of the
> imagination and of the artistic faculty.
>
> And sometimes what waxes strong is the thirst of the
> emotional faculty in purity of the heart and inlonging
> of the spirit.
>
> And sometimes what waxes strong is the thirst for
> study of what can be expressed in books, in letters
> and in words.

One type of thirst is the **thirst for Divine enlightenment** – for abstract, philosophical ideas, for profound issues of faith and spirit; another kind of thirst is artistic thirst, expressed as the desire of man to make things tangible for himself, to create works of art, to write and sing, to express the life of his soul in a variety of modes; in addition to these is thirst for learning, the desire to encompass in depth large sections of the Torah.

> And it happens that all of these thirsts wax strong
> together, intermingling in the faculties of the heart,
> merging together in different combinations, and
> a perfect harmony of holy melody emerges from
> them.

This is a unique description of the situation where different kinds of thirst come together, and this state can only be reached by a person who is alert, attentive, and honest with himself. Those who possess this thirst are awarded not only a subjective experience but also attain a special logic distinguished by a profundity of ideas, to which this thirst leads. To possess such a thirst and such inner self-awareness, to have a desire for inner-directed development and refinement of the quality of one's spiritual life – is both a privilege and an achievement.

E. Thirst for knowledge of G-d

Here we arrive at a more general phenomenon, man's thirst for knowledge as such. This thirst can be seen as a widespread human characteristic; people are thirsty to know, to comprehend, and to learn. There is a connection between the spiritual thirst which we have discussed until now and the thirst for knowledge that exists in all of mankind – man's desire to know the world in which he lives, to know the wisdom behind the natural reality, to better understand human beings and the makeup of the human soul.

In Rav Kook's journals, 'Eight Notebooks', we learn that these two kinds of thirst – spiritual thirst and thirst for knowledge – go hand in hand[11]:

> **Science in general is the adjustment of man's spirit to all of reality.**

Rav Kook perceives science as a process that takes place between man and the world. Man was created on the sixth day of creation, so that he arrived in a world that was already built. In man who was created, there stirs a spirit – the image of G-d – and out of his unique spirit, from his unique inner world, he encounters the external world. This world does not always cooperate with man, does not always operate as we would want. Therefore, there is a need for an adjustment process, this process lasting as long as human history, when mankind tries to adjust to the world and to get along with it. Man encounters the world and learns what it is

---

11 **Shmona Kevatzim**, I, 811.

that he faces. The world has many laws – some of them immediately evident and some of them hidden – and man must adjust himself to these. In this perspective, history can be seen as the process of man adjusting to a given reality.

Rav Kook goes on to distinguish between the two types of knowledge, practical and spiritual:

> **Practical knowledge is ready to teach him ways of acting in his life based on this adjustment [to the external world], but the role of spiritual knowledge is greater than this: to complete the spirit of man so that he will not be detached from the world surrounding him, so that he can draw upon all of existence to receive vital, spiritual sustenance, for only then will he find his existence complete.**

Practical knowledge deals with the physical dimensions of reality, with the laws of nature, and undoubtedly the development of this part of knowledge helps man manage in the world more successfully, whether in terms of medical knowledge, managing his life, or in other ways. It is easy to see that the development of practical knowledge, what we call science, is part of the adjustment process, because it is very pragmatic and its effects are clear and obvious.

However, above this is pure knowledge, **spiritual knowledge**, which does not have a pragmatic purpose but is rather the process of learning and recognition from the perspective of the higher truth for which the world exists. The development of this part of knowledge is also a process of adjustment: by dint of this knowledge, man is less disconnected from the rest of the world, he feels more at home in it, and as a result, he is able to "draw upon all of existence to receive vital spiritual sustenance". There are many things that one can take from the world, and the better we know it in terms of science, the better can we absorb new modes of thinking and different systemic structures and our learning becomes more sophisticated. Ultimately spiritual knowledge also has many practical, though less immediate, implications, for many things in our daily life are influenced by the way the world operates, to the point where Galileo Galilei said "Mathematics is the language in which G-d has written the universe". The very orientation of thought of pure science, according to which there is a general law from which many individual details are derived, has implications for many individual aspects and instances in our lives. These implications relate not only to how we "get along" with the world but to the very way that man, through science, perceives some of the wisdom concealed in reality.

That is the secret of the thirst for knowledge, whose pinnacle is the thirst for knowledge of the light of G-d, the light of G-d which is the basis of all existence, and of more than all existence, infinite with no end.

Thirst for knowledge is, in effect, man's thirst to live a more perfect life, less detached from existence; the highest expression of quenching this thirst is in the knowledge of G-d, because this knowledge helps us confront the undercurrents and constitutive order of life, until we find in our lives more depth and wholeness. Studying Torah, engaging oneself in the word of G-d, means learning the rules with which the world was created. Reality has a more profound basis than that which can be realized and measured with physical instruments. There are **moral** principles upon which all of existence is built , and in fact – they **are** existence. The desire to know the Torah is the pinnacle of the thirst for knowledge, because through the Torah we encounter the highest values, the principles on which all of reality is built, and in the words of the sages: "G-d was looking in the Torah and creating the world"[12]. In the profoundest sense, contemplating the spiritual treasures written

---

12 **Gen. Rabba** 1:1. **see Tzaddik B'emunato Yihye**, 140, and nos. 4-6.

in the Torah is in fact contemplating the world and ourselves, and through the Torah, we desire to receive much more from the world than we would have had had we not been given the Torah.

We thus learn that there are three tiers in the relationship between knowledge and the world:

Practical knowledge which deals with teaching man to cope with the world in a pragmatic sense.

Lower spiritual knowledge whose province is teaching man to absorb from the world insights and ways of thinking.

Higher spiritual knowledge, knowledge of G-d, whose province is teaching man to receive knowledge of G-d from the world, because the world is built according to the same spiritual principles that we encounter when we reconize the light of G-d in the Torah.

F. Roi's thirst for knowledge and life

Rav Kook ends by saying that the highest level of adjusting to the world is adapting oneself to 'He who spoke and the world came into being':

> **The most important demand of the spirit is for man to adapt himself to the true reality, to existence as a revelation of G-d, and that is the secret of the highest labors performed by those who are righteous of heart, who rejoice in the knowledge of G-d and delight in the glory of His name.**

These highest labors are very difficult. A person can succeed at them only if he has within him the fiery flame that we discussed earlier. As much as it is difficult to bring to light the laws of science which are hidden from the eye, it is still even harder to bring to light the spiritual laws that form the foundation of reality. The upright in heart who are privileged to perform this highest labor of sanctity are rewarded with gladness, as it is written : "Light is sown for the righteous, and gladness for the upright in heart"[13]. Gladness in knowledge of G-d is a special kind of joy; it is not the gladness that comes from letting loose, from venting one's feelings but rather one of constant alertness and vibrancy, of perpetual enthusiasm, of a very high level of vitality. In the pleasure of the quest, learning, and exploring, in the pleasure of exposing a more profound, more transcendent truth than was previously known, there is something that is sweeter than anything else. This is the delight that causes one to ignore the sense of passing time, the delight when one doesn't feel the hours slip away and the books piling up high. And thus pass days and weeks, months and years, and this delight is only at its beginning because within the heart is the thirst to know and understand, the true passion to know the truth in full, and until everything is totally clear and precise – it is still not enough because we have not yet arrived at the true law on which everything is built.

During my studying with Roi I was privileged to learn in this way, to learn with an approach not satisfied with half-truths or partial explanations; because Roi had in him a powerful thirst, a passion lit with a lovely fire, to see things organized and understood, to arrive at an understanding of each subject in full, even if completing our investigation took weeks and even months. He toiled and developed within himself boundless patience, which enabled him to wait until everything, point by point, was in its proper order, until the true order would reveal itself.

To reach the level of diligence and love of Torah that Roi did is possible only when a person is motivated by a powerful thirst. This thirst develops as a result of an education that encourages

---

13 **Psalms** 97:11.

curiosity, the desire to know and to understand the world. This kind of education begins in childhood but it must continue throughout one's life. The ones who succeed will be those who learn to appreciate the quest and not just the achievement, the effort and not just the result.

In Roi we were privileged to see a very varied and rich thirst. He was thirsty not only for book-knowledge but for a life of completeness, for perfecting himself and the world around him and for honesty, for developing a diversity of life forces. His thirst gave rise to very powerful energies, to very high, almost extreme, demands he made of himself, and within all of this – to an amazing serenity, patience, and joy. Let us try to adopt into our own lives Roi's thirst to receive the Torah in the wilderness, in fire, and in water.

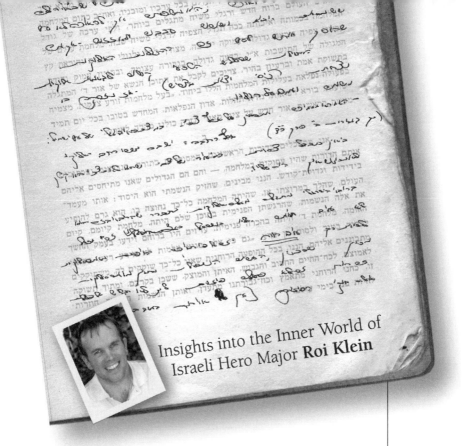

Insights into the Inner World of
Israeli Hero Major **Roi Klein**

Chapter 3

Moon and sun: Balancing renewal and stability

Moon and sun: Balancing renewal and stability

A. Moon and the sun in the Hebrew calendar

B. Progress and rest as complementary principles

C. The tent and the dwelling, moving and resting

D. Between Shabbat and the festivals

E. "This month shall be for you" – Time is ours

F. Shabbat – permanent and unchanging

G. The people of Israel were compared to the moon

H. Early mornings with Roi

A. *Moon and sun in the Hebrew calendar*

Tonight celebrations and parties are being held all over the world and unfortunately, also here in Israel[1], to mark the civil new year. That is why I thought that it would be an appropriate time to talk about our calendar, the Hebrew calendar, while in the background will remain our objective of acquainting ourselves with another aspect of Roi's character as I was privileged to know it.

The Hebrew calendar is very complicated due to the fact that it is built on a formula that integrates both the earth's orbit around the sun and the orbit of the moon around the earth.

The calendar used by most nations, eastern and western alike, is the Gregorian calendar, based exclusively on the cycle of the sun, i.e., on the period in which the earth completes a full circuit around the sun. The cycle of the civil year is quite fixed, and there is typically a correlation between the date and the season of the year: December will always be in the winter, and May, in the spring.

The Moslem calendar, in contrast, is based on the lunar cycle,

---

1   See **L'Netivot Yisrael** [Hoshen Lev 5758 ed.], III, 232 ["The new civil year"].

i.e., the period in which the moon makes a full circuit around the earth. A year based on this cycle is eleven days shorter than a solar year. Since the Moslems refrain from intercalating the year, i.e. declaring 'leap years', over the course of a few years a large discrepancy develops between their year and the solar year, and so Moslem holidays can fall in different seasons, because there is no connection between their calendar and the seasons of the year.

Our Hebrew calendar integrates both of these systems. We attribute great importance to the lunar month, which is expressed in the commandment to sanctify the month and counting the twelve months based on the new moon. On the other hand, we have a commandment written in the Torah: "Observe the month of the Aviv [spring]"[2]. This commandment requires us to take pains that the holiday of Passover will always occur in the spring, and, as a corollary, the holidays of the month of *Tishrei* will always occur in the fall. The balance between these two requirements obliges us to declare a leap year seven times within a cycle of nineteen years, making a significant intercalation by inserting an entire month into the year. This is in contrast both to the Gregorian calendar where there is a leap year only once every four years in which a single day is added, and to the Moslem calendar where there are no leap years at all.

B. Progress and rest as complementary principles

Beyond the role that the sun and the moon play in determining cycles of time, they also symbolize for us two different states of the soul, two different spiritual focal points around which our lives revolve.

When we enter the synagogue in the morning, it is customary to recite the verse: "How goodly are your tents, o Jacob, your dwellings,

---

2   **Deut**. 16:1. See also **Ex**. 23:15; 34:18.

o Israel"[3]. In his commentary on the prayer book, "*Olat Reiyah*", Rav Kook discusses the difference between the two seemingly similar expressions: 'tent' and 'dwelling'[4]. These expressions are parallel in that they both describe a place of residence, but there is a difference between them. Using this difference, Rav Kook analyzes two key principles in the spiritual development of every person:

> **The blissful self-perfection for which a person should constantly strive throughout his life without pause, is based on two fundamental aspects, comparable to foundations that serve as a base to all that is delightful in the world.**

In order to reach what Rav Kook calls here "that which is delightful in the world", a person must keep in mind at one and the same time two separate calculations:

> **The one [aspect that must be kept in mind] is the highest pinnacle of every good quality, so that a man should always strive to elevate himself, to rise higher and higher in his level of sanctity, to add wisdom and knowledge of all that is holy, to be illuminated by the light of the radiance of the knowledge of G-d and of his power, by the light of purity and sanctity that comes through additions of wisdom and knowledge, through purifying one's feelings and thoughts, through strengthening constantly one's nobility of spirit.**

It is obvious and natural that when dealing with character development, one needs a strong will to move ahead, an ambitious nature. The ambition to make progress is essential whether the subject is learning, or moving up in the levels of purity and sanctity, or refining one's feelings, or, in general, elevating one's soul to a

---

3   **Num.** 24:5.

4   **Olat Reiyah**, I, 42-42, s.v. "Ma tovu oholeha".

state that is nobler than its preexisting one. It is no less important, however, to take note of another principle as well:

> **And the second [aspect that must be kept in mind] is the foundation on which the position is built, that which guards against destruction, that is in fact the content that maintains the desire to elevate oneself, that gives rest to its highest waves, and provides a place of rest for the soul (neshama) lest it venture destructively beyond its capacity.**

The second thing that one must emphasize is the ability to preserve achievements that we have already made. In every field, one can arrive at impressive achievements by dint of strong ambition and concentrated efforts, but these achievements can be dissipated because of lack of attention to the need to maintain them. If we do not take pains to preserve the achievement, to establish and to maintain it, we will find ourselves slowly losing it. As with everything in life, so too it is in the field of the spiritual. Just as there is a need for spiritual progress, there is also a need to preserve spiritual achievements. There is a certain tension between these two ambitions, because in order to preserve what already exists, one must make a decision not to invest effort toward advancing but instead, in stabilizing the status quo. We must ensure that what we have achieved through our labors shall indeed remain ours, and not became some fleeting experience that we had in the past without retaining from it something that we internalized.

However, while it might seem that the aspiration to preserve stands in opposition to the aspiration to progress, in fact it is precisely this ability to preserve that gives meaning to the next stage of progress. Because when does a person see true meaning in his advancement? Only when he knows that every step forward does create something in his character, that the achievement that he has made through great effort adds a stable and genuine new level to his spiritual stature. It is only then that there is significance in taking another step forward towards perfection, and setting new aspirations for himself.

This perception sheds light on the concept of "rest". Usually rest is perceived as something marginal, necessary for accumulating strength between activities. However, we see that the holiest day for us, the Shabbat, is a day of rest. If rest is nothing more than a means, how has the day of rest become the high-point of our week? The answer is that the purpose of rest is not only in order to accumulate strength before the next phase of progress but also to **gather, establish, and preserve all of the achievements to date.**

Rest of this type is sublime! Man's success becomes meaningful only when he has put what he has achieved on a firm footing. For example, a person can read a book at lightning speed, but the real question that he must ask himself is what true acquisition has he retained by reading the book. Full possession comes through rest. This is true not just in studying; a person can engage in volunteer work with all of his strength for a certain period and that is admirable, but the question is whether he can continue to do so with perseverance.

"You rule the raging of the sea; when the waves rise up, you quiet them"[5] – it is exactly when the waves rise up to impressive heights, that one must know how to stabilize them. It is precisely when one reaches high spiritual levels that there is a need to make use of the principle of rest, which holds the secret of stability. Without it, there is a danger that spiritual thirst will cause anarchy and breakdown.

---

5   **Ps**. 89:10.

C. The tent and the dwelling, moving and resting

Rav Kook now draws a parallel between the spiritual foundations that we have mentioned and the two kinds of structures mentioned in the verse, the tent and the dwelling:

> "The tent" and "the dwelling" are two names for a place of residence that may be prepared for journeys, journeys which represent in the highest spiritual sense, the longed-for ascensions.

> The tent symbolizes the principle of motion, the aspect of preparation that accompanies travel, aimed always toward change and ascension, accompanied by the most sublime bliss, in the direction of the Divine radiance.

> The dwelling place, though also connected in some way to preparing for a journey, represents the aspect of rest between journeys, and – in the soul of man – it is the calming feeling that halts incessant movement in order to firmly establish the higher goal, preserving the light and strengthening its foundations in place.

The tent is temporary and folds up quickly, and it therefore represents the element of **movement**. The dwelling, in contrast, is a structure characterized by permanency within the transient situation of the desert, and is therefore identified more with the element of **rest**. The tent parallels the element of aspiration for spiritual elevation, while the dwelling is the element of rest when we establish, internalize, and assimilate all of the spiritual wealth that we have accumulated during the stage of spiritual elevation. There is a certain tension between these two elements in the soul. For example: Anyone who engages in the study of Torah knows that there is a tension between the desire to learn new things and the need to review that which has already been studied, something which takes time away from what could be used for progress; it is the same in other aspects of life. How delicate is the balance that we must strike between these two demands!

The balance between the tent and the attending principle of movement and the dwelling place and the attending principle of resting is parallel to the balance between the sun and the moon. The moon is characterized by movement, the moon waxes and fills out until it reaches its fullest stage, but immediately after it has become perfect and round, the waning begins. That is the reason that we call the cycle of the moon the 'hodesh'[=month], from the word *hit-hadshut*, which means 'renewal'. We do not – G-d forbid – worship the moon, but we do try to learn from its patterns whatever can be learned about the world of our soul; the moon serves as a reminder of the momentum of renewal that is embodied in us. The sun, on the other hand, expresses what is permanent and clear: "There is nothing new under the sun"[6]. The sun is portrayed as a focal point of permanency and stability, and that is why the natural world revolves around it to a large extent.

On the verse in Numbers that describes the additional sacrifices brought on Shabbat and the new month (*musafim*) "This is the burnt offering of every month throughout the months of the year"[7], Rav Kook writes in *Olat Reiyah*:[8]

> **The attribute associated with the idea of the month is the recognition of the newness of the Divine light which expresses itself in the fresh appearance of the festivals from a transcendent place which is above the sun, a place where newness flows freely and frequently, in contrast to what is under the sun, of which it was said "there is nothing new".**

6 Ecc. 1:9.
7 Num. 28:14.
8 *Olat Reiyah*, I, 165, s.v. "Zot olat hahodesh".

Just as times renew themselves, so does man's spiritual life. Within our personal world, within our set of desires, we can and must find an element of movement and renewal. However, in order to develop oneself, in order for this renewal to have something to lean on, there is a need for a regular routine, symbolized by the cycle of the sun. Just as we need both the tent and the dwelling, we likewise need to focus our attention both on the months and on the solar year. The most perfect achievement is to reach a new spiritual-moral achievement and afterwards to work to make it second nature, a permanent principle established firmly in our lives. Success in this is also a source of encouragement for further spiritual elevation and renewal.

D. Between Shabbat and the festivals

The difference between the sun and the moon is also reflected in the fundamental difference between the two kinds of holy days: the Shabbat as opposed to the festivals. Shabbat is determined according to a count of seven days, seven settings and risings of the sun, and therefore it is related only to the sun. On the seventh day, when the sun sets, Shabbat enters. The moon has no influence upon when Shabbat begins, because it is tied only to the solar cycle. In contrast, the festivals are fixed according to a certain date[9], and the dates depend on the first day of the new month (*Rosh Hodesh*). Who decides when *Rosh Hodesh* falls? We do. The people of Israel decide what day is *Rosh Hodesh*, based on the status of the moon. While nowadays one can calculate what day the new moon will be, using the calendar instituted by Hillel the Second (the fourth generation *Amora*), the proper, preferred situation is one where we determine the festivals by looking at the cycle of the moon.

---

9   Editor's note: While the holiday of Shavuout has no fixed date, since it begins fifty days after the day after *Pesach*, and *Pesach* is determined in accordance with the sanctification of the moon, it too is ultimately connected with the system of sanctifying the month, i.e. the cycle of the moon.

This idea is novel but it is fact: The people are the ones who decide the time of the festivals through the *Sanhedrin**, which is the spiritual leadership that represents them. The well-known mishnah in tractate *Rosh Hashana*[10] describes an instance where Rabbi Yehoshua, who was probably the greatest of the sages in terms of his abilities, calculated that Yom Kippur should fall on a certain day. However, the *beit din* under the leadership of its president, Rabban Gamliel, calculated another date. This is not a negligible controversy because the resolution of this question determines when the fast of *Yom Kippur* should be observed, or G-d forbid, when it will be considered desecrated. Rabban Gamliel told Rabbi Yehoshua that, with all due respect, the people, through its authorized representative, the *Sanhedrin*, had decided otherwise, and therefore: "I order you to come to me with your walking stick and money, on the day that according to your calculations is *Yom Kippur*". By doing this it will be clear to all that *Yom Kippur* does not fall on the day decided by an individual rabbinical sage, as eminent as he might be, but rather on the date established through a decision made by the public's representatives. After difficult soul-searching, Rabbi Yehoshua did go to Rabban Gamliel as he was asked to, on the day that he had maintained was *Yom Kippur* according to his calculations.

E. "This month shall be for you" – Time is ours

As I mentioned previously, the fact that it is we, human beings, who decide when the festivals fall is a great revolution in thinking. In the *mishnayot* (pl. *mishnah*) of tractate *Rosh Hashana*, there is a very vivid and graphic description of the process of sanctifying the month. On the twenty-ninth day of every month, everyone looked

---

10 **Mishnah**, *Rosh Hashana* 2:7-8.

* the supreme council of Israel, consisting of 71 sages, was the supreme court (*beit din*) and legislative body in all matters of Torah law.

skyward and sought the moon. In order to do this, they had to wait until a certain hour close to sunset, because it is hard to detect the new moon while the sun is still shining, and even at this hour, the moon can only be seen as a hair-thin sliver in the sky. The first two witnesses who managed to identify the moon would rush to the *beit din* in Jerusalem; that they were permitted to desecrate the Shabbat in order to travel there testifies to the importance of the matter.[11] The witnesses rushed to the *Sanhedrin* to report that they had seen the new moon, i.e., the new birth of the moon. But what in fact had been born? **Time was born.** But has not the moon been traveling in its orbit for thousands of years already? Here we must understand the deeper meaning: the message of the renewal of the moon is that we human beings are also capable of experiencing renewal. The nation's spiritual leadership, the *Sanhedrin*, determines the beginning of the month based on testimony by witnesses, and this decision determines when *Yom Kippur* will fall when we must fast, and when *Pesach* will fall when we must refrain from eating bread. The Master of the Universe determined the existence of the date, but exactly when that date falls – that is another matter: it is in our hands.

When the Torah informs us that it is up to us to make the decisions pertaining to the ordering of times, this means that "Time" as such is ours to determine. This statement includes not just a compliment but also a quintessential definition of the concept of 'Man'. What is 'Man'? An entity that holds time in his power. Entrusting us with the ordering of time puts a great responsibility

---

11 Editor's note: This is even more striking in light of the fact that the Tanaim (Mishanic sages) were in dispute over it [see tractate Rosh Hashana 1:5); Rabbi Yossi thought that the Shabbat should be desecrated only if the moon were seen in a way that was not "obvious", not clearly visible to every observer, and his reasoning was that it is precisely then that there was a concern that if witnesses would not desecrate the Shabbat to reach Jerusalem immediately – the month would not be sanctified. However, the law was decided according to the first opinion, according to which, even if the moon is seen clearly by all – the Shabbat must be desecrated to give testimony, and this is despite the fact that it is nearly certain that by the time the witnesses who are desecrating the Shabbat arrive in Jerusalem there will already be local witnesses who arrive at the *beit din* before them.

upon us; it teaches us that time does not pass by us but is actually within us. We have the power to shape time, to decide how it shall be used, and as a result: how all of our life shall be shaped. Time contains an infinite number of opportunities, and the decision as to what will be done with the time that is in our trust is, in fact, the decision about what to do with the gift of life. The fact that a person does not know in advance how much time he has only adds to the challenge. The bit of **life** belonging to an individual and to a society is the **time** that has been entrusted to them.

The moon, in the freshness of its emergence and in the daily changes that take place in it, contributes to our understanding of the concept of time. Time expresses freedom. It must be treated in the sense of freedom and liberty, because the decision as to what to do with it is totally free. Not everything is predetermined and known in advance, as the determinists' mantra would have it; man has the freedom to choose what he will do with the time and with the life he was given.

Against this background we can understand why the first *mitzvah* that the nation was given as a nation is the *mitzvah* to sanctify the month:

> *This month shall be to you the beginning of months; it shall be the first month of the year to you.*[12]

Even before the exodus from Egypt, Moshe and Aharon receive a command whose subtext is this: **You** decide about time. Liberate yourselves two weeks **before** you escape the social status of slavery, because true liberation does not begin with the question of economic class[13] but rather with the decision that time is yours, life is yours, and from the moment you understand this, **you are**

---

12 **Ex**. 12:2. Also see **Rashi**'s commentary on Gen. 1:1 according to which it would have been appropriate to begin the Torah with this verse.
13 According to *Olat Reiyah*, II, 245.

already a free man. The moment you know what renewal is, you are no longer like a stone thrown before the wheels and cogs of existence unchanging and predetermined in their motions like the solar system and the laws of nature that repeat themselves endlessly, unalteringly, without innovation or novelty. You are different, you are a human being, and Man is special in having time given to him; it is even possible to take a unit of time and to uplift it by deciding that it is holy! Many qualities of ours as human beings begin and end with the question of time, and therefore this is the first G-dly aspect that we encounter just before we are about to leave Egypt.

In his talk on *parashat* 'Bo' where the commandment to sanctify the month appears, Rav Zvi Yehuda Kook deals with the subject that we are discussing[14]:

> **The first commandment is to sanctify the month. "This month shall be to you the beginning of months". This commandment is connected to the sanctity of the festivals, and it is unique to Israel. "This month shall be *to you*...". It is Israel who sanctifies the festivals. Time is a wondrous thing and many scientific and philosophical studies have been written about it. Time is a strange thing, that cannot be felt with the fingers like space but it is where the reality of man and the world exist. Time is not something that has a reality of its own, but the fact of our reality is found within it. Man who was created in the image of G-d exists in this world, and time is the order in which Man's life is arranged in this world. The appearance of the soul (*neshama*) within the body in the order of history – is the subject of time. Time is Man in the world.**

14 **Sihot Harav Zvi Yehuda** on Shemot, pp. 132-133.

Time does not exist in itself, but is part of a formula: Man, in the image of G-d, appearing in physical reality equals time. If we could take ourselves out of the world, one could say that there would be in effect no time. A famous Jew once even defined time as a matter of attitude, of relationship, of relativity.[15] Everything focuses on the question of one's relationship to life and reality. What time do we define as 'precious time' or alternately as 'wasted time'? It is all a matter of attitude. Time is not as objective as it seems at first glance.

F. Shabbat – Permanent and unchanging

We have already mentioned that the sanctity of Shabbat is essentially different from the sanctity of the festivals. There is no need for a *Sanhedrin* and witnesses in order to determine that the Shabbat has arrived; we do not decide its time.[16] The sun sets and rises with mechanical precision, and the seventh day rolls around. In the language of the Talmud: The Shabbat is "fixed and permanent".[17] It will come whether we like it or not. The Shabbat expresses another fundamental principle: "When Shabbat comes – rest comes"[18].

Shabbat does not deal with renewal, freedom, and liberty but with another question altogether: Man, what are you left with after all of your renewal? What has become your spiritual property? About

---

15 The reference is to Albert Einstein's theory of relativity. It is interesting to note that Rav Kook met Professor Einstein in 1923 and showed him an ancient source from the *Kabbalah* that supports the theory of relativity, see R. Simcha Raz, "**Malachim Kivnei Adam** (A Biography of Rabbi Avraham Yitzchak Hakohen Kook), pp. 376-377 [Hebrew, 1st edition].

16 .Editor's note: Still, in **Mei Marom** IV (commentary on the Passover Haggada), p. 80, Rav Harlap states that the people of Israel will ultimately reach the level where they will be capable of renewing even the sanctity of the Shabbat. Also see the comment by Rav Bezalel Naor in *Aviv Ha-olam*, p. 221, no. 336.

17 **Talmud Bavli**, *Pesahim* 117b; *Hullin* 101b.

18 *Tosafot*, Sahhedrin 38a.

what can you say sincerely: "This is mine"? You moved about in the physical reality, you ran here and there, you were very free – excellent! And now, what have you taken with you from all of that? At the end of all the processes you have experienced, at the end of all of the renewal, who are you really?

When a holiday begins on Saturday night at the end of Shabbat, there is a special version of the *havdala** that we recite: "You have distinguished between the sanctity of the Shabbat and the sanctity of the holidays" and it ends: "Blessed are you O G-d who distinguishes between holiness and holiness". What kind of distinction is being made here? It is the distinction that exists between the tent and the dwelling, or between the sun and the moon, and one must bear in mind these two fundamental principles all the time, in parallel.[19]

G. The People of Israel were compared to the moon

An individual has the power of renewal, and no less important – a nation has this power. We have already mentioned that in fact it is the nation of Israel that sanctifies the months, and the members of the *Sanhedrin* were acting as its representatives in this capacity.

---

19 In **Sihot Harav Zvi Yehuda** on Shemot, p. 133:
"The holidays are called holy by us, by the *beit din*. "These are the appointed festivals of G-d, the holy convocations which you are to declare in their appointed times" – it is you who are to declare them. But Shabbat is not dependent on a *beit din*, it is "the Shabbat for G-d", "Therefore, G-d blessed the seventh day and sanctified it". The Shabbat is not our creation, it is "Shabbat kodesh", "shabbat the holy", possessing its own absolute holiness from the time of creation. "The Shabbat of Creation does not require the act of sanctification of the beit din", as the festivals do. The sanctity of the festivals is a second level of sanctity, which is declared by us, by virtue of the Torah that is within us. It is necessary to distinguish between these two levels of sanctity. "You have distinguished between the sanctity of the Shabbat and the sanctity of the holidays... You have distinguished and You have sanctified ...Blessed are you O G-d who distinguishes between holiness and holiness". The sanctity of the festivals is generated by Israel. It is G-d who sanctifies Israel and by virtue of this, Israel sanctifies the festivals."

* Havdala – the service that marks the end of Shabbat.

A nation that sanctifies the moon is not only expressing by this act the desire of a great many separate individuals to renew themselves but the desire of an entire nation for renewal, **as a nation**. We are a very 'old' nation, ancient in historical terms, but for all that, a nation which manages to renew itself and to give expression to the fresh forces within itself, and thus the nation remains young and does not grow weary. Its future is still ahead of it and it is always interested in new things. We very much want to be a young nation, not because we do not respect age but because we want to progress. Therefore, in describing the aspirations of the nation, we frequently use the moon as a parable, as Rav Kook writes in 'Orot'[20]:

> **Knesset Yisrael (the People of Israel as a single ideal expressing itself throughout history in each generation of Jews) is compared to the moon, at times its fullness is shattered and at times it is built up, at times it is full and at times it is but a crescent, and during the times when it is in its vanishing phase, when it reaches the end of this waning...**

There are times that the nation reaches a situation which is expressed in a sense of national deficiency and decline, but it is precisely when one comes to the feeling that the moon has nearly vanished completely that it begins to renew itself:

> **Ready and waiting just behind the wall is the replenishing of its light, so that it continues to fill up, until it reaches that condition of strength where the light of the moon will be like the light of the sun, and it will never again be in a state of deficiency but rather it will always be full of light.**

Every fresh appearance of a new month, should serve as a reminder to us that we have the power to renew ourselves. Even in times of decline, we never hit rock bottom. For example, it is hard to

---

20 **Orot**, Orot Yisrael, 7:6 (pp. 162-163).

grasp this but a mere three years after the Holocaust, the state of Israel was born. What are three years from a historical perspective? Nothing at all, an insignificant speck of dust. Could there be any point lower, more abased, than the point that we reached during the Holocaust?! But the power of growth and renewal is planted very deep in our national character and we must believe in this power and know that the moon will ultimately be built up, even arriving at a state where its fullness will be permanent, as we pray when we recite at *Kiddush Levana* :

> *May it be Your will my G-d and the G-d of my forefathers, to fill the deficiency of the moon, and to make it that there be no lessening in it, that the light of the moon be like the light of the sun and the light of the seven days of creation.*

We pray that the renewal and the culmination that we attain, "the light of the moon", be enduring and stable in our lives, acquired by us as a possession in its own right – "like the light of the sun"[21].

H. Early mornings with Roi

Striking a balance in our lives between these two aspects, between renewal and stability, is very delicate work. A balance between the joy of living, energy, and ambition on the one hand, and integrity, permanence, and seriousness on the other – is a task that requires much patience. But this difficulty is an integral part of the aesthetics of the attempt to arrive at the correct balance, a balance whose very existence proves that we are dealing with something that is alive and complex, containing within many diverse things. On the one hand, every day is new and on the other, our lives are also comprised of the attributes of perseverance,

21 See **L'emunat Itenu**, I, p. 18

consistency, order, seriousness, and discipline, elements that in another context could be portrayed as stagnation and monotony. The interaction between the character of each day – new, full of surprises, interest, and happiness, and the human quality of insisting on perseverance and stability, avoiding gratuitous shocks, entering a routine and sticking to it – is very real and profound. It is very tempting to open new vistas all the time but great *gevura* (here: strength of will) is also required to achieve a balance, so that we are responsible for all of the horizons that we open up, so that we can point to our attainments as genuine, so that they are able to endure.

These cold days flood me with memories relating to the subjects that we have been discussing. On our way here from our home in Eli, we drove very slowly due to the heavy fog very typical of our neighborhood that made visibility difficult. This trip reminded me of my trips with Roi in the early morning when it was still dark outside – part of our daily routine. On those days we would drive down very slowly from our neighborhood to the *bet midrash* in the center of the *yishuv*, many times in a pouring rain. Every morning, faithfully, we would arrive at the *beit midrash* at about five thirty in the morning, a commitment that required persistence and self-discipline. And thus we would arrive in the dark, privileged to be the ones who turn on the lights in the *beit midrash*, where it was still freezing cold, and we had an hour and half until the beginning of morning prayers. Because of the bitter cold, we couldn't sit down, so we would stand with our hands in our pockets, and Roi would jump up and down in place to warm himself, all the while also trying to read the words of the Talmud, and to discuss the subjects that we were studying. How special were those mornings when we were alone in that great *beit midrash*... Those two aspects, renewal and stability, that we are discussing, would flow together as one on those mornings and fill them. On the one hand, we would study on a daily basis, every day, at the same hour and under the same conditions, over a period of months, and on the other hand – renewal: every day and its own special matter, whether the jokes of the morning, the keen interest in approaching a new topic, a new talmudic issue, or sometimes to take up with renewed attention a subject that we had set aside the day before. Never was it boring, never was it dull, it was always very challenging, always full of adventure; and it all came from within, without the need for any external aids. From these powerful memories, I try to take the courage of will just described, and the ability to continue in the unceasing effort to achieve a balance between the sun and the moon, between movement and responsibility, preservation and application, to find the equilibrium between the great ambition to study more and more of the Torah and the need to repeat, review, and persevere.

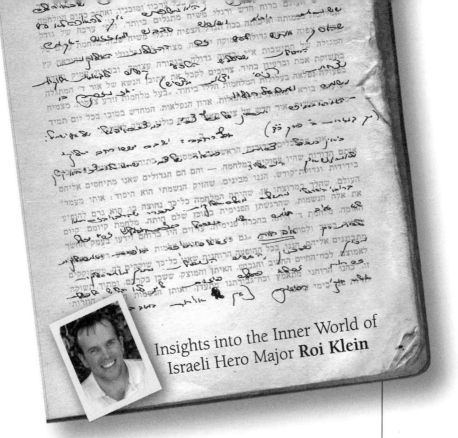

Insights into the Inner World of
Israeli Hero Major **Roi Klein**

Chapter 4

The joy of emulating Hashem's ways

The joy of emulating Hashem's ways

A. The unique character of each month

B. The letter kuf – like an ape (kof) before man

C. Imitation that is uplifting and elevating

D. Divine mirth

E. The merriment of the month of Adar

A. The unique character of every month

The month of Adar approaches, and in one of the notebooks that Roi left, I found a summary of a lesson given four years ago, that deals with the nature of this month. The summary is very concise and we shall use it to try to understand what we learned together then.

A book called 'Sefer Ha-yetzira' is an important source for understanding the essence of the months of the year, a source belonging to the esoteric section of the Torah. In this book there is a list of the zodiac signs for all of the months, the letter of the alphabet that represents the idea of each month, and a quality in the human soul that corresponds to the nature of that month. From the very composition of this kind of list we learn that a month is not an arbitrary division of time, devoid of meaning, but rather a unit of time that bears a particular significance that should be highlighted.

We tried to decipher the specific esoteric allusion attached to each month and in that way to understand its unique character. One of the sources that helped us greatly was a book by Rabbi Zadok of Lublin on the *parasha* of the week, known as '*Pri Zadik*'. In this book Rabbi Zadok relates frequently to the special character of each month and to the esoteric nature of each of them. The summary that we are using reflects an attempt to decipher the esoteric nature of the month of Adar.

The letter that *Sefer Hayetzira* attributes to the month of Adar is the letter 'kuf' (ק), and the quality associated with Adar is mirth. It is not difficult to understand why mirth is associated with the month of Adar more than other months, because that is when we increase our level of joy (*marbin b'simẖa*). However, we must understand the value that mirth embodies: what is the profound spiritual meaning of laughter. As to the zodiac sign of the month of Adar – we must clarify the connection between Adar and Pisces (fish), and the meaning of the connection between Adar and the letter *kuf*, the quality of mirth, and the zodiac sign of Pisces.

B. The letter kuf – like an ape (kof) to man

Let us start with the letter kuf. The name of the letter is very similar to the Hebrew word for ape – "kof". In tractate *Bava Batra*, we learn about something very important that one can learn from the ape:

> **Man in the presence of the Shechina (Divine Presence)**
> **– is like an ape in the presence of man.**[1]

The Divine Presence is the revelation of G-d in the world, from which man must learn as much as possible. Our status vis a vis the Divine Presence should be like that of the ape vis a vis man. Besides the obvious message placing the Divine perfection much, much higher in the hierarchy than man with all of his weaknesses, there is a possibility of understanding the words of the Talmud to mean that man should **imitate** the *Shechina*, in the same way that the ape imitates (apes) man. The ape makes motions and gestures that remind us of human behavior prompting some to observe that a man imitating others is behaving like an ape. It is appropriate for man to imitate his Creator just as the ape imitates the human

---

1   **Talmud Bavli**, *Bava Batra* 48a.

being. In the words of Rabbi Zadok:

> **Chazal taught (in Bava Batra 58a) that "Man in the presence of the *Shechina* – is like an ape in the presence of man", that the primary basis of the mitzvot is "and you shall follow in His ways", because to create the world G-d emanated words of Torah and commandments with which he conducts His world, and He commanded Israel to follow in His ways.**

The objective of the Torah which we were commanded to study and of the commandments that we were commanded to perform is to awaken us to follow in the ways of G-d. We want to emulate the ways of G-d to the best of our abilities. As Roi wrote at the end of his summary:

Kuf (the letter) – kof (ape) to become holy.

We want to resemble the sacred, the Holy One Blessed Be He (G-d).

In the next line he wrote:

The base aspect of the ape – the mimicry of externals. The high aspect of aping – Just as He is compassionate, so should you be compassionate; just as He does acts of hesed (undeserved kindness), so should you.

The unbecoming aspect of imitation is easily understood, it is its superficiality. What is new here is the idea that there is also a positive kind of mimicry, when we emulate the attributes of G-d; this kind of mimicry is the best thing that a person can do in the world. It allows him to extricate himself from the restricting bonds he is subject to by the very fact that he was created. It is only by setting before him a totally different superior standard that a person is able to rise above his present world of conceptions. This process begins with externals but gradually becomes more internalized and builds man's inner world. The whole purpose of our spiritual development is to follow in the path of G-d and to understand it insofar as we are able.

Here Roi wrote down an idea that we raised as we studied together, and I remember it as though it were yesterday, how his face lit up with joy at this insight:

> The eye of the needle is called in Hebrew a 'kof.
> The verse " **Open for me a door as big as a needle's eye**"[2] can be seen to imply that the basis of teshuva is to be a kof (needle's eye - to ape).

If the needle's eye is called a *kof*, one might say figuratively that if we were only a bit like *kofim*, if we would only imitate the Creator of the Universe, He would help us return in complete *teshuva*. That must have been what Roi meant when he wrote that the basic element of *teshuva* is to be a *kof*...

Further on in his book, Rabbi Zadok notes that it is written explicitly in the Torah that the reason for resting on Shabbat is that G-d "rested" from all of His work on Shabbat. Here, too, one may see that our goal is to emulate G-d:

> **And regarding the commandment of Shabbat which encompasses all other commandments of the Torah, the reason for resting is stated outright: because that is when I rested; so too all of the commandments – to try resemble G-d in our ways, i.e. acting like an ape in the presence of the *Shechina*.**
>
> **And for Israel, the letter *kuf* alludes to the word 'kadosh' (holy) [as stated in Talmud Bavli tractate Shabbat 104a], and it is written "Holy shall you be,**

2   Abridged version of the sages' words in **Song of Songs Raba**, beginning: Kol Dodi: "The Holy One said, open for me a door as big as **a needle's eye** and I will open for you a door through which wagons and carriages may enter".

> because I am Holy", and our rabbis taught (Midrash Tanhuma on parashat Kedoshim): "Since you were sanctified in My name, therefore be holy as I am".

The fact that we are human, so infinitely distant from G-dly perfection, brings about a situation where only by imitating the ways of G-d can we attain holiness.

Rabbi Zadok ends thus:

> And the month of Adar, the last month of the year, was created with the letter *kuf* which alludes to the holy, which is concerned with "Holy shall you be, because I am Holy", and that is the aspect of the *kof* (ape), to resemble G-d, as it were, and that is the holiness demonstrated on the part of Israel.

C. Imitation that is uplifting and elevating

Rav Kook in his commentary on the letter *kuf* adopts an approach similar to that of Rabbi Zadok. This commentary appears in a slim volume called "Rosh Milin" which is written – in contrast to Rav Kook's other books – in a style that is distinctly esoteric. In his book, Rav Kook analyzes all of the letters of the alphabet: the basic idea they embody, the name given to the letter, and even their written form. These commentaries are based on the idea that letters in Hebrew are not merely graphic symbols but a kind of narrative, a way of transmitting a message. For example: the first letter, the one that enables us to begin studying, is called *aleph*, which means to educate and teach, as in the words derived from it, like *ulpan* (classes for teaching Hebrew) and *ulpana* (school).

Regarding the letter under discussion, the letter *kuf*, Rav Kook writes:

> The *kuf* shows the trait of imitation, which is described as an ape vis a vis a man, which has a basic element of holiness, to have man and every level of reality striving to resemble that which is above them and in doing so, they elevate and uplift themselves.

The first steps of constructive mimicry come as a result of turning our attention to that inner voice that says to us that we are capable of changing and being, to some extent, somebody different than we are at present. Anyone who changes, especially if he does so by his own initiative, is torn between his genuine desire to change and his desire to remain faithful to himself as he is now, and not to pretend that he is someone else. When a person first starts to make a change in himself, it is hard not to feel that there is something forced and unnatural accompanying his attempt to change. However, on the other hand, the knowledge that a person is capable of improving his character and making a change, that he is not doomed to always remain in the same situation and status, gives purpose to life and is a source of consolation and hope. In our ability to change ourselves, we elevate and uplift ourselves

Let us skip to the end of the Rav's words on the letter *kuf*:

> Imitation that is pure, that contains a noble ideal, has the ability to elevate those who are low, from the very lowest depths to the heights of holiness, the holy *kof* (ape).

Even when one has reached the lowest level, still, when we see someone whom we want to emulate or when we encounter an ideal that we want to rise up to attain, man has the ability to elevate himself from the lowly situation where he is and to reach the highest levels of holiness.

D. Divine mirth

After understanding the idea behind the letter *kuf*, let us try to understand the connection between it and the zodiac sign of Adar – Pisces, or fish. Further on in his summary Roi wrote:

In Adar, there is also the element of the fish – the leviathan* – mirth.

The connection between the fish and the leviathan is clear, what is less clear is the connection between these two elements and mirth.

We shall begin our investigation of this subject with the verse in the book of Psalms, where merriment and the leviathan are mentioned together:

"This leviathan you fashioned to play (be merry) with".[3]

According to this verse, G-d created the leviathan for His amusement. Needless to say, this is a very bizarre statement: Is the ocean an enormous bathtub in which the Creator of the Universe – G-d forbid – needs a leviathan to play with?!

This astonishment is compounded by the words of the *aggadata*** in the Talmud, which purport to describe the "daily routine" of the Holy One. The gemara states[4]:

There are twelve hours in a day. During the first three hours the Holy One Blessed be He sits and studies the Torah;

3   **Psalms** 104:26.
4   **Talmud Bavli**, *Avoda Zara* 3b.
* According to the Midrash, the leviathan is a giant fish, created by G-d on the fifth day of Creation, which rules over all the creatures of the sea.
** The part of the Talmud given over to a homiletic interpretation of Biblical verses – primarily focusing on understanding Jewish ethics and profound ideas from these Biblical sources.

during the second three He sits and judges the whole world, and when He sees that the world is guilty and deserves to be destroyed, He rises from the Throne of Justice and sits down on the Throne of Mercy, [and mercifully He decides to spare the world and treat it with leniency];

during the third three hours He sits and feeds the whole world, from the mighty re'em [rhinoceros or wild ox] to the smallest insect;

during the fourth three hours He sits and plays [is merry] with the leviathan, as it says, "This leviathan You fashioned to play with".

It is obvious that G-d's daily routine as described here is an allegory describing the way G-d rules the world. The Maharal explains this gemara[5], and this is how Roi summed up the Maharal's explanation as we learned it:

Torah – the Divine order of reality. Busy studying Torah – The Torah is at all times the inner order of reality.

Justice – the individual instances and the application of all of the highest values that are embodied in the Torah, according to which reality is conducted.

Feeds – Gives existence to reality.

The connection between the Divine essence and the world – playful merriment with the leviathan, the great sea creature – the word leviathan comes from the root l'v'h', **to accompany**, to connect with. This merriment is the will of G-d to be connected with His creatures.

---

5   **Hiddushei Aggadot l'Maharal**, Avoda Zara p. 24 (Hoenig & Sons Ed.)

Let us try to explain this:

He sits and studies the Torah Reality has its own rules of physics, but above and beyond these, are the spiritual laws, laws that G-d established in order to rule the world and to bring it to the Divine Good. The Torah is the order of reality. It teaches us the internal principles according to which reality operates, and the actions mandated by the commandments of the Torah are those which express these principles.

He sits and judges the whole world – Divine justice is the particulars and application of the highest values that appear in the Torah.

He sits and feeds the whole world – The Holy One Blessed be He created the world in such a manner that it will persevere and endure, and so that all of man's shortcomings – both practical and moral – can not have the power to cancel out G-d's plan, which ensures the existence and progress of the world.

He sits and plays [laughs] with the leviathan This is the part that is relevant to our subject. It is related to mirth. The Maharal explains the word 'leviathan' as 'accompaniment', as the word is used in the book of Job[6]. [This also calls to mind Levi, the third son of Leah, who was given this name because of her explanation that when one has two children, the mother can still hold them in her hands, but when there is a third, she needs her husband to accompany[7] her to manage the third child].

Let us examine the language of the Maharal:

> It is called the leviathan as in: (Proverbs 1:9) "a graceful garland [l'viyat chen] for your head and chains around your neck". The term here refers to something that

---

6   See **Job** 3: 8 and the commentaries there.
7   According to **Hizkuni,** Gen. 29:34.

accompanies and is connected, because this creature is unique in having the Divine will connect to it... and that is how it is related to mirth, because there is nothing that expresses a connection like merriment.

The thing that most expresses a connection and belonging is merriment, which appears when a person is very happy with something. "Then our mouth will be filled with laughter", the expression of an ideal situation where joy flows without any need for effort.

And since people thought that merriment is a matter of mockery and nonsense, they were alarmed by these subjects. But the true sages did not agree with them, because mirth is none other than the Absolute Will that is united with its creations and that is mirth. Because our sages in their wisdom extract the essence of the matter, the essence of mirth, and the essence of mirth is none other than the connection and the conjunction of the Will with the object of the mirth.

The Creator of the Universe wants to establish a tie with us and to accompany us, and when the sages say that He laughs playfully with the leviathan, they refer to this will. Mirth, which reflects empathy and a very great spiritual bond, comes to teach us that G-d is very "happy" in His connection with us. We have already learned that we for our part want to be mimics, and now we see that G-d, too, helps us in this by being, as it were, very interested in having His attributes emulated and the Divine Good fill the world. Therefore He accompanies us, "lending a hand" to connect to us and to help us imitate Him.

The next sentence written by Roi is based on a saying of the sages[8]:

> *" Ever since the Temple was destroyed, there is no merriment in the world."*

In light of the words of the Maharal, we understand that this means that relative to the strong connection that existed between G-d and the world during the period that the Temple stood, the situation today is one of detachment, as though there were no connection between G-d and us. The possibility of imitating someone depends on the extent of the connection with him, and when the connection is broken, there is also a difficulty in imitating him, because his image gradually fades away.

E. The merriment of the month of Adar

Roi writes:

> *Apes – the highest clowning. Man's instinctive psychological connection is to laugh. It can be base and it can be lofty, an exalted union.*

The will of G-d to have a connection with us expresses itself in revelation which makes it possible to imitate Him, and this is the greatest joy that can exist; this is merriment. "When the month of Adar begins, we increase our level of joy"[9]: the arrival of the month of Adar together with the idea that is associated with it – that one can make genuine changes in one's life and be a mimic of something that is so great, and that G-d on His part is also happy that we are imitating Him, and even helps us to do so – there is no joy greater than that! That is why we masquerade in this month. The disguise is a reflection of the will that we have within us to be

---

8 "Ever since the day that the Temple was destroyed, there is no laughter for the Holy One blessed be He." **Talmud Bavli**, *Avoda Zara* 3b.

9 **Talmud Bavli**, *Taanit* 29a.

somewhat different, to change, to imitate the Divine greatness by attaching ourselves to His ways.

Small children have a natural desire to imitate. When a little child is given an opportunity to "dress up" like someone else, he will choose to masquerade as the hero he admires. Childish imitation is instinctive; children are always learning by imitating others, but what the child does instinctively, the adult must do deliberately, by making a conscious choice of the figures that he wishes to be like, or of the values that he admires and wishes to adopt.

The last sentence of Roi's summary:

Yitzhak (Isaac) renounced everything in the presence of the Divine Will.

Our forefather Yitzhak, whose name incorporates the Hebrew word for mirth (*tzehok*) is the personality who reflects more than any other the total connection with G-d. Yitzhak is a man who is prepared to give everything and even to be sacrificed, and this attribute corresponds to his name: his willingness to renounce everything in the face of the Divine Will, and to emulate as much as possible the Creator of the Universe, holds the greatest happiness and that is what generates 'holy laughter'.

The pinnacle of the merriment which is so much associated with the month of Adar is *Purim*. *Purim* marks the first time in the history of the Jewish people that the nation was successful in being a genuine imitator of the Holy One Blessed be He. Until *Purim*, our relationship with G-d was very simple: He commands, and we carry out His orders. On *Purim* we decided by ourselves, for the first time what we had to do, and we even made the right decision! Throughout the *megilla**, there is no mention that G-d commanded us to read the *megilla* or to send each other gifts of food. Furthermore, the

---

* scroll read on *Purim* retelling the miraculous rescue of the Jewish people.

name of G-d is mentioned nowhere in the entire *megilla*. All of the *mitzvot* relating to this day, including the very fact of establishing it as a day of rejoicing for posterity, are decisions that we, the Jewish People made by ourselves. What's more, we are even "compelling" G-d, as it were, to be a partner to our decisions, because we recite the blessing "Who has sanctified us with His commandments and commanded us to read the megilla". Our self-confidence in our own power of imitation is that great! *Purim* represents the high point of trust reached in our relationship with the Master of the Universe, a trust so great that the one being commanded allows himself to replace the Commander momentarily, and this is the ideal state of mirth, accompaniment, and connection.

Our joy on *Purim* derives from our ability to do *teshuva*. In our traditional sources there is a comparison drawn between '*Purim*' and '*Yom Kippurim*'[10], and implied in this is that even *Purim* relates to the subject of *teshuva*[11]. On *Purim* we understand that it is possible to be different from what we usually are, and that we can free ourselves from the rigid, restricting outer shell; if we use this holiday properly, it can facilitate new ways of thinking about our path in life.

In Roi's notebook one can see that he underlined the words: "external mimicry" and "will". What is emphasized is the contrast between casual imitation and imitation that leads to a true change of human will. Just as the relation between these contrasts is one of

---

10 **Tikkunei Zohar**, Bo, 57b.

11 "And now [on *Purim* – ed.] through happiness, one can reach the stage of doing *teshuva*, a stage reached on Yom Kippur through affliction". **Sefat Emet,** *Purim* 5636, "Bepurim".

opposition, so, too, are there two opposite types of merriment: the hilarity of emptiness, as opposed to the joy that a person experiences because he is progressing, because he is moving forward and developing his character, a happiness with the perfection that is his.

Roi was filled to overflowing with the second kind of happiness, a joy that comes from setting for himself a very high standard and from his ability to meet that standard. This kind of happiness is not born of levity but of the joy of a soul-connection with ideals of sanctity. This is the kind of happiness that the Talmud writes is necessary to have in order to merit prophetic inspiration born of a connection to the Divine Glory[12]. Let us pray to merit that kind of happiness, a happiness that stems from the sense of privilege that we have been accorded, that we are able to resemble the Master of the Universe.

12 **Talmud Bavli**, *Shabbat* 30b.

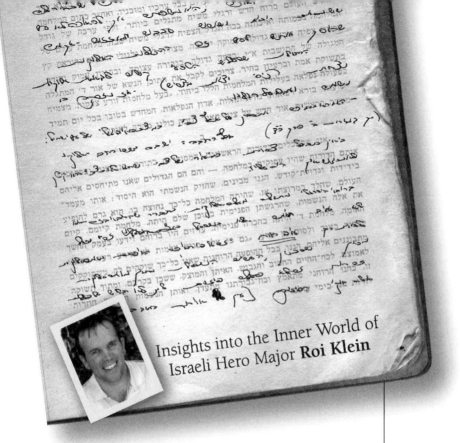

Insights into the Inner World of
Israeli Hero Major **Roi Klein**

Chapter 5

In humility lies the secret of Redemption

In humility lies the secret of Redemption

A. Do we mention the Exodus from Egypt at night?

B. The Exodus: an act of G-d alone

C. The Exodus and the final Redemption

D. Jacob and Israel; cause and effect

E. True humility

F. Humility as a fundamental of Jewish nationhood

A. Do we mention the exodus from Egypt at night?

The Passover *haggada* quotes from the Mishnah the following rabbinical dispute, a dispute that seems somewhat perplexing at first glance:

> *Rabbi Elazar ben Azaryah said: "I am like a man of seventy years old, yet I did not merit having the exodus from Egypt mentioned at night, until Ben Zoma explained it: "It is said, (Deut. 16) `That you may remember the day you left Egypt all the days of your life;' `the days of your life' refers to the days, [and the additional word] `all' indicates that the nights are also included!"*

> *The sages, however, said: "`The days of your life' refers to the present-day world; and `all' indicates the inclusion of the days of Mashiach."*

The subject of this discussion is whether the exodus from Egypt should be mentioned at night, as the third section of the 'Shema'.

Rabbi Elazar ben Azaryah was surprised by Ben Zoma's words according to which the Exodus can be mentioned at night. Until that time Rabbi Elazar had theorized that the Exodus was a subject fitting only for the day, for the new morning that dawns. The night arouses associations of darkness and gloom, both physical and spiritual, appropriate to the period of exile and slavery much more than to the exodus from Egypt. However, from the word 'all', a word that is used to include an item that otherwise would not have been taken for granted, Ben Zoma infers that the Exodus should be mentioned at night, too.

The sages dispute this conclusion and explain the verse differently: in their opinion, had the word 'all' not been written, we might have thought that it is only in our time that the Exodus must be mentioned; however, during the days of the Mashiach, which will eclipse the Exodus with their splendor, the story of the exodus from Egypt will be supplanted and disappear from our consciousness. The verse teaches us something we would have otherwise not recognized, namely: even then the Exodus will retain a place of honor in our national and spiritual consciousness, and we will continue to mention it.

The *haggada* does not record Ben Zoma's opinion on the issue of mentioning the Exodus during the days of the Mashiach, but the Talmud in tractate *Brachot* [1]completes the picture:

> *The Breita teaches: Ben Zoma replied to the sages: Do we indeed mention the exodus from Egypt in the days of Mashiach? It has already been stated (Jer. 23): "Therefore, behold, the days come, says G-d, that they shall no more say: 'As the L-rd lives, who brought up the children of Israel out of the land of Egypt'; but: 'As the L-rd lives, who brought up and who led the seed of the house of Israel out of the north country, and from all the countries into which I had driven them'".*

Ben Zoma marshals support for his opinion from the verse which states explicitly that the ingathering of the exiles will usurp the

---

1   **Talmud Bavli**, *Brachot* 12b.

special position and status of the exodus from Egypt.

The sages counter his argument thus:

> *They said to him: The exodus from Egypt will not be totally supplanted but (our redemption from) forced submission to the gentile kingdoms will be primary and the Exodus will be of lesser importance in comparison.*

While the Exodus will be demoted from the central position it presently occupies to a lesser status, it will not vanish **completely** from our consciousness and we will continue to evoke it forever.

As stated previously, this argument seems a bit peculiar: what possible interest could we have today (or in the time of the Mishna) in the "troubles of the rich", i.e., with the question of how – in the future after the Mashiach finally comes – the status of the Exodus will be regarded? This astonishment only increases in light of the evidence that the sages bring to bolster their theory:

> *Similarly you say: (Gen. 38): "Your name shall no longer be called Jacob but your name shall be Israel".*

After an entire night that Jacob struggled with the angel, he demands that the latter bless him, and the angel informs him that the name Israel will replace his present name Jacob[2]. However, later on in the book of Genesis, we see that despite the fact that 'Israel' has become his chief name, the name Jacob continues to appear in parallel to it[3]. True, our sages maintain that just as the name Israel is primary but the name Jacob did not disappear, similarly in the future the Full Redemption will be primary but the exodus from

---

2   That is what he was told by the angel in **Genesis** 32: 28 and afterwards he was told again by Divine revelation in **Gen**. 35:10.

3   In fact, even after his name was changed to 'Israel', the name 'Jacob' appears in the Book of Genesis more times than the name 'Israel'.

Egypt will remain important. Still we must clarify **the intrinsic** connection between the two names of our forefather Jacob and these two historical events.

An explanation for this subject appears in the writings of the Maharal of Prague.

B. The Exodus: an act of G-d alone

Roi and I spent a lot of time studying the works of the Maharal (Rabbi Yehudah Loew of Prague, 1512-1609). The Maharal is an illustrious figure in the Jewish world who was noted for his profound Torah knowledge as well as his erudition in other areas. The Maharal was admired by the entire Jewish people, and many legends and tales have sprung up around him, among them the famous story of the "Golem of Prague" which he created. The Maharal was a Talmudic genius and an important *posek* (decisor of religious law), who is mentioned several times in the commentaries on the *Shulḥan Aruch*. However his major contribution to posterity is the unique books that he wrote on Jewish philosophy and belief. The Maharal developed a well-organized and profound system of Jewish thought, and he wrote in a style that is unparalleled. There are those who deem his central works to be "the trilogy" – *'Gevurot Hashem'* – on the exodus from Egypt; *'Tiferet YIsrael'* – on the giving of the Torah; and *'Netzaḥ Yisrael'* – on the exile and redemption of the Jewish people. Roi and I studied his book *Tiferet Yisrael* together, and we began *Netzaḥ Yisrael*. After Roi returned to the army, we would manage sometimes to continue to study this book together on Sundays, early in the morning, before he returned to the army after Shabbat leave with his family.

In his introduction to *Netzaḥ Yisrael*, the Maharal deals with the Exodus as the basis for our hope of the Redemption. On the first page of Roi's notes on *Netzaḥ Yisrael*, the follow summary

appears. Let us try to use it to deepen our understanding of the
subject and the role of the exodus:

> Studying the exodus from Egypt is actually
> studying where the Jewish people came from –
> not of natural need but through Divine revelation.

Studying the exodus is not a study of history but the study of
ourselves. From the story of the beginning of the People of Israel
we learn that we did not consolidate as a nation in a gradual
process. Our leaving Egypt was not the result of natural processes
of becoming disillusioned, establishing an underground insurgent
movement, collecting weapons and the like, but was rather the
result of an act of G-d, who chose us and took us out of Egypt, as
stated in the Passover *haggada*:

> **We were slaves to Pharaoh in Egypt, and the L-rd, our
> G-d, took us out from there with a strong hand and
> with an outstretched arm.**

> **If the Holy One, blessed be He, had not taken our
> fathers out of Egypt, then we, our children and our
> children's children would have remained enslaved to
> Pharaoh in Egypt.**

And later on in the *haggada*:

> **"The L-rd took us out of Egypt," not through an angel,
> not through a seraph and not through a messenger,
> instead the Holy One, blessed be He, did it in His glory
> by Himself...**

> **"I will pass through the land of Egypt," – I and not an
> angel;**

> **"And I will smite every first-born in the land of Egypt,"
> – I and not a seraph;**

> **"And I will carry out judgments against all the gods of**

Egypt," – I and not the messenger;

"I am the L-rd," it is I, and none other!

The creation of the People of Israel is an act of G-d alone, for which we ourselves cannot take credit[4]. Not only did we not take action in ways that could have brought about our exodus from Egypt but we were also incapable of carrying out such acts.

> The Jewish people consolidates its identity emerging from the nutrient-rich soil of a family, the family of Jacob which recognizes clearly that it is not a nation; it is a family but on the face of it, not a nation. Six hundred thousand, and we are slaves and not budging – but what turns them into a nation is the Divine revelation.

The Children of Israel live in Egypt with the consciousness of being a large family, a 'clan', but without any national awareness.

Although we are speaking about a population that numbers six hundred thousand men, in other words a population of a few million people, they have no national identity, they are just a very large band of slaves somewhere in Egypt; a group of people who are not lifting a finger to change their situation, but rather are enslaved and passive, unable to do anything to the point where the passage of the *haggada* quoted above declares that had not G-d taken us out of Egypt, we would never have left.

Seder night is our "birthday", a day when we rejoice greatly and emphasize that it is not we who performed this miracle but that it all happened in a way that was not natural, in a miraculous act of creation by G-d.

---

4   See **Olat Reiyah**, II, 287 ["Matza"].

C. The Exodus and the final Redemption

Let us continue to read Roi's summary:

> *Revelation that the natural world is connected to eternal Divine objectives (the miracles of the exodus from Egypt) - it was then that a soul (neshama) was injected into it and it stood on its feet.*

The exodus from Egypt, with its miracles and wonders, does not just bring about our nationhood but also demonstrates that the natural world is not detached from the Creator of the Universe. G-d wills a nation to be created that will know and serve Him[5], and the laws of nature itself are mobilized to help with this mission. The ten plagues, as well as the other miracles of the Exodus, occur so as to teach that the appearance of this nation in history is a matter of Divine involvement. The process of the Exodus infused a soul into this collection of slaves, and it became a nation.

Only by understanding the unique nature of the appearance of this nation can we understand its confidence and certainty in its future and renewal. This is a nation which is ruled by laws different from those that govern every other nation and people. Other nations collapse and crumble when they go into exile, while the people of Israel endures here today after two thousand years of exile. Do you want to understand the historical strategy of the people of Israel, the miracle of its existence, survival, and renewal? Go to the source, to the beginning! There you will discover that the very structure of our identity is fundamentally different. A nation that is formed naturally – is also dependent on natural circumstances, and these circumstances require that every nation undergo a historical process which ultimately ends in its decline and exit from the stage of history. But we were formed differently:

---

5   According to **Moreh Nevuchim**, III, 51.

This is what has stood by our fathers and us! For not just one alone has risen against us to destroy us, but in every generation they rise against us to destroy us; and the Holy One, blessed be He, saves us from their hand[6].

This – the promise by G-d to our forefather Abraham in the covenant* with him, that his descendants would become a nation and inherit the land of Israel.

The Holy One, blessed be He, saves us in every generation because from the very beginning, He created us in a supra-natural way with a mission that is essential to the perfection of the world[7].

Now we can understand the profundity of the rabbis' reply to Ben Zoma: We can not generate any optimism about our national future without mentioning the past, without a reference to the exodus from Egypt. Our ability to be certain of G-d's salvation in the knowledge that the days of the Mashiach will surely arrive, springs only from the power of the Exodus. Without the connection to the Exodus, there are no days of the Mashiach. The day that we attribute all of our national accomplishments to ourselves is the day that we lose the major source of hope and optimism in our lives. Because if our success in the past is the result of our own deeds, who will guarantee that we will succeed in the future as well? However, in contrast to man, whose powers are finite, the Divine source is infinite, and He who gave us strength to succeed in the past will also give us the necessary strength to succeed in

---

6   From the Passover *Haggada*.

7   "We began to say some great thing, to ourselves and to the entire world, and we have not yet finished saying it. We are now in the middle of our oration, and we are neither willing nor able to stop...Leaving the stage of history is possible only for a nation that has finished what it began, for a spiritual vision that has actualized all of its hidden potential exposing it to the light of the world." **Orot**, *Zar'onim* VIII, p. 136.

* "the Covenant between the Pieces" made with Abraham, see Gen. 15.

the future; He who redeemed us from Egypt in the past will also redeem us in the future.

Let us examine this idea as it appears in the writings of the Maharal[8]:

> The sages are of the opinion that the Exodus will be recalled in the days of the Mashiach, too, because how is it possible to mention the effect without reference to the cause?

Our hope has a source, and one cannot possibly talk about hope for the future without mention of the source for it.

> Because it is from the spiritual eminence that the people of Israel attained when they left Egypt, that they later attained also a still more exalted eminence, and if G-d had not removed us from Egypt and taken Israel for His people, they would not have merited that exalted eminence that they will attain in the future, because the exodus from Egypt is an essential cause of the future Redemption.

The high point that we achieved when we left Egypt is the source of our optimism regarding the future; we know that it was our Father in heaven who took us out of Egypt, and it is He "who will redeem us once again in the sight of all living things, in the end as He did in the beginning" (from the *musaf* prayer).

D. Jacob and Israel; cause and effect

In order to reinforce their argument, the sages provide evidence: although Jacob was told that he had a new name – Israel – the

8 Introduction to **Netzaḥ Yisrael**.

name Jacob was not forgotten but rather continues to be used in parallel to Israel. But what is the connection between the changes in Jacob's name and the matter that we are studying?

To understand this, one must note that Jacob's two names have opposite meanings. Jacob was called by this name [יעקב] because at birth, he emerged holding the heel (in Hebrew, akev [= (עקב] of Esau[9]. Someone who hangs onto another person's heel is usually visualized as a follower, someone who strings along after a more dominant personality. Jacob is, then, a name that would seem to express a lower level, an insignificant personality. The name Israel, in contrast, comes from the root word of 'serara' – mastery or power: "Because you have contended with angels and with men and you have prevailed"[10]. "You have contended" – the Hebrew word 'sarita' is related to the word 'sar', a leader, a figure of authority. On the one hand, a name expressing dependency and insignificance, and on the other, a name that reflects leadership and power. Therefore we would expect that when the angel tells Jacob that his former name has been revoked, and from then on he is to be called 'Israel', he would jump at the chance as if he had found a great fortune because he is finally ridding himself of that ignominious name that expresses weakness and dependency. But we see that this is not the way things actually are, and from this we understand that the name 'Jacob' has a role to play not only in Jacob's past but also in his future, and that this name does not gainsay his new name 'Israel'. Why then the need for two names and what is the relationship between them? Let us return to the Maharal for the answer:

> **As evidence the Talmud brings the name of Jacob and Israel. The name Jacob was not eliminated because the name 'Jacob' was also the cause of the name 'Israel'. He was called Jacob because he would**

---

9   **Gen.** 25:26. And in **Rashi**'s second comment ad. loc.: "His father called him Yaakov (Jacob) because he held onto the heel [= akev]".
10 **Gen.** 32:29.

humble himself assuming a level of insignificance as low as the heel of a foot, and there is nothing in a person lower than the heel, and this is the cause behind G-d's elevating him to the level where he is called Israel, because "you have contended with angels and with men"(Gen. 32:29), because whoever humbles himself, the Holy one blessed be He raises up (*Eruvin*, 13b).

Because of those attributes expressed by the name 'Jacob', Jacob merited the name 'Israel'. 'Jacob' is not an ignominious name but rather one that denotes a spiritual state essential for creating the still higher level – that which is expressed by the name 'Israel'. Jacob was a person who belittled his own importance. He left the house of Lavan with tremendous wealth, which he had accumulated through hard labor and prodigious sophistication. He does not, however, attribute his achievement to himself but rather to G-d.[11] Jacob did not mind being small, in a psychological state of humility, and it was precisely for that reason that G-d raised him up, and he was deserving of the name 'Israel'.

These points must be considered carefully. Why does G-d raise up those who humble themselves? Is it a kind of compensation or gift? Do the sages want to encourage us to self-abasement carried out for the purpose of achieving glory afterwards, G-d forbid? Here we must contemplate the issue of humility and the true meaning of this attribute. It was said of Moshe that he was the humblest of all men on the face of the earth, and in general, we see that the great leaders of our nation were characterized by a large measure of modesty and humility, among them men of unquestionable leadership abilities like our forefather Abraham, who said of himself: "But I am ashes and dust" (Gen. 18:27) and Kind David, who said "But I am a worm and no man, a reproach of men and despised of the people" (Ps. 22:7). How can you be a ruler and leader, even a

---

11 **Gen**. 31:9; 33:11.

king, and yet diminish and debase yourself? Here we touch upon a very significant issue and when we come to speak of Roi, it is perhaps the most important one: what is true humility?

E. True humility

Later in his summary, Roi wrote of our forefather Jacob who diminished himself:

> *He doesn't diminish himself because he is of no value, or because he is empty of significance but because he has a perspective that causes him to attribute whatever he has to its source, not to himself.*

The statement "I have nothing to recommend me, I am nothing, I am worthless" is not true about most people and certainly when said about great, gifted people like our forefathers and those who were our leaders at the beginning of our history. Every person possesses some wisdom, talent, and ability. There is nothing positive in the statement "I have nothing to recommend me". True humility is the recognition that I do have much in me **but none of this is mine**. Did the person of intelligence invent his own intelligence? Did the possessor of great physical strength achieve his strength by himself? Did the artist create his own artistic and creative talent that he was gifted with? Each of the talents that we possess has a source, and the humble person is he who acknowledges the truth, who knows what life forces he possesses and at the same time – is not proud, because he attributes all of these powers to He who created them, the Master of the Universe. Humility is placing things in their true light: talents which we did not create but received from the Divine source give us no reason to be vain. It is not man's recognition of the talents he possesses that is defined as arrogance but rather identifying the source of these gifts as himself.

*That is why " G-d raises him up" - he fills with
devotion to G-d, he fills with every good quality.*

Devotion to G-d is the connection of that which is created with the
Creator, the connection of that which is created with its source.
A humble person is always reminding himself of his connection
to the Master of the Universe and by doing so, he becomes truly
connected to Him, and remembers that the source of all of his
powers and talents is G-d. The humble person creates devotion to
G-d at all times through his very approach to life.

Now a comment appears in parentheses, probably because
these are Roi's own thoughts and not part of the summary of the
lesson:

*When a person is arrogant, when he inflates his
self-importance, when he attributes [strengths] to
himself, as a natural result he sets himself up vis a
vis the Holy One blessed be He and he is a nothing,
he cuts himself off from devotion to G-d.*

In this light, we can understand why the rabbis have compared
pride to idol worship[12]: this is an approach to life that cuts off
its proponent from devotion to G-d, because it leads a person to
worship himself instead of G-d, the source of life[13].

---

12 "A person who is haughty – it is as though he worshipped idols…Rabbi Yohanan
said: as though he denied the existence of G-d…Ula said: as though he had built an
(unlawful) altar …". **Talmud Bavli**, *Sota* 4b.
"Rabbi Elazar said: A person who is haughty – deserves to be chopped down like a
tree…Rabbi Hisda, and some say Mar Ukba, said: "Of any person who is haughty, the
Holy One blessed be He says: He and I are unable to exist [together] in the world".
Talmud Bavli, *Sota* 5a.
"A person who walks even 4 cubits [the minimum distance] with his head held high,
is considered as though he had encroached upon the Divine Presence." **Talmud
Bavli**, *Brachot* 43b.

13 "…And that is why our sages have said that haughtiness is equivalent to actual
idol worship, because the root and essence of idol worship is considering something
to be an entity existing independently of G-d›s sanctity…" **Tanya**, end of chapter
22.

The Maharal goes on to explain:

> **And that is why the people of Israel were also given these two names [Jacob and Israel], because when they make themselves small, G-d raises them up. And because that is the case, both of the redemptions [from Egypt and the final redemption] are connected as though they are actually one event of redemption.**

We never abandoned the name of 'Jacob' because it continues to be connected to us always. The name 'Jacob' signifies humility and diminishment of self-importance, a psychological foundation essential to attaining devotion to G-d, the devotion that recognizes that it is G-d Himself that is raising us up. Now it is clear why this perspective is **very much** related to the relationship between the exodus from Egypt and the days of the *Mashiach*, as Roi wrote in his summary:

Here we find an essential connection to the Exodus, to the creation of the Jewish Nation.

The constant connection to the exodus from Egypt is also by definition our link to the understanding that our formation as a nation is not an act of human beings originating from below, in the historical realm, but rather it is G-dly, initiated from above, and it is for that very reason that we have the certainty that He who took us out of Egypt will also redeem us in the future. It is precisely by diminishing ourselves – something that a superficial understanding would claim is debilitating – that we connect to our source of strength and power. A person linked to the Divine source, who acts out of a sense of Divine mission, in humility, receives powers that no one other than himself has. The Divine source gives him life.

F. Humility as a fundamental of Jewish nationhood

Continuing these notes, Roi wrote a very pertinent definition :

The exodus from Egypt – the phenomenon of humility as a national phenomenon. The people of Israel – are humble.

Seder night is an evening that is total humility. We look at the extensive history of the people of Israel and say: It was not our hands that brought about this miracle. Therefore, fittingly, on this night we eat humble bread – matza, that thin, slight bread that does not have a drop of air in it, that is not puffed up; a bread that is minimal, free of pretension. How fitting to this night is the declaration that we make: "Let all who are hungry come and eat". Is all of this abundance that I have been given my own, that I can keep it only for myself?!

The results of humility: the arrangement and discovery of all of the talents and all of the powers until man in all his stature realizes his full potential.

Roi's definition of humility as a national characteristic is very exciting. This definition should also have an impact on each and every individual. The quality of humility teaches the individual and the nation to pay attention to what they receive, both during periods of redemption as well as during periods of exile. The Passover *haggada* was recited by Jews throughout the generations even in exile and under conditions that were far from normal. From it Jews throughout the generations knew that the present they were living was not the whole picture, that the day would come when the people of Israel would rouse themselves and return to their homeland, and the superpowers of the world which seemed so omnipotent – would decline and fall.

Engraved in my memory is the story of Yehoshua Cohen, one

of the leaders of the Lehi underground*, who hung a picture of the bust of the Roman emperor Hadrian in his home. When he was asked to explain, he replied that it served a purpose for one day in the year – the ninth of Av, a day of mourning commemorating the destruction of two Temples and the exile of the Jewish nation. On that day, Cohen said, he used to console himself by looking into the eyes of the statue while murmuring: "Hadrian, Hadrian, where are you now and where are we..."[14].

14 Editor's note: The Roman emperor Hadrian brutally suppressed the Bar Kochba Revolt and destroyed the greater part of the Jewish community living in the Land of Israel. The combination of the crushing blow that he dealt us and his extreme cruelty is what earned him the epithet attached to his name by the sages 'shehik tamiya' – may his bones be ground to dust.

* Lehi ("Fighters for the Freedom of Israel") was a pre-State Zionist underground that fought the British for unrestricted immigration of Jews and the creation of a Jewish state.

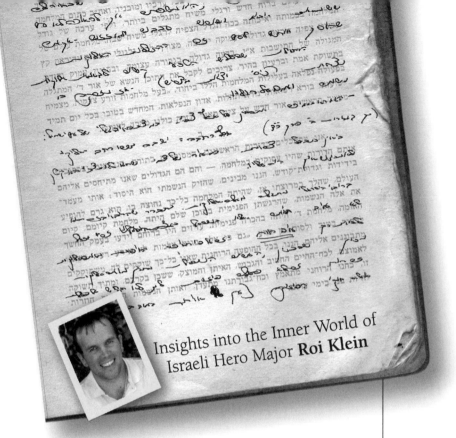

Insights into the Inner World of
Israeli Hero Major **Roi Klein**

Chapter 6

Israeli heroism (*gevura*)

Israeli heroism *(gevura)*

A. Heroism of body and soul

B. Heroism whose source is honesty

C. Heroism in war as an act of benevolence

D. Heroism is tested in periods of transition

E. Rabbi Nehunya ben Hakanah

F. "The joyful song of Your people"

G. "Those who remember Your holiness"

H. The entreaty and the cry

I. The heroism of perseverance

J. Roi's heroism

A. Heroism of body and soul

This lecture opens with a dilemma: there was a request that we talk about the attribute of *gevura**, and another request that we study '*Ana Be'koah*', a prayer whose words appear in the song used to accompany the film made in Roi's memory. The problem was solved after I discovered in a book that I was studying that the subject of the prayer '*Ana Be'koah*' is the attribute of *gevura*, and so the two subjects – are actually one and the same. Let us then begin with a discussion of the attribute of *gevura* by itself, and afterwards deal with a number of aspects of the subject of *gevura* as they are given expression in the prayer '*Ana Be'koah*'.

In Roi's *gemara* notebook, dating back to the time when he first

---

* "*Gevura*" in Hebrew means the ability to persevere, the capability to maintain a resolute stand in the face of obstacles or opposing forces. Depending on the context, this capability can be translated as: heroism, strength, power or courage. When talking of G-d's attributes, "*gevura*" refers to setting definitions and limits that stand unyielding against forces otherwise unbounded. We shall translate *gevura* variously as the text requires.

arrived at the beit midrash for graduates of the pre-army program in Eli, there is a single page with a summary dealing with different sources relating to army service. The first source mentioned is the explanation given by Rav Kook on the Mishnah in tractate Shabbat:

> *A person shall not go out [into the public domain on Shabbat] either with a sword, or with a bow, or a shield, or a cudgel, or a spear. If he goes out with any of these, he is required to bring a sin offering. Rabbi Eliezer says: These are his ornaments.[1]*

The Mishnah states that a person should not go out of his private domain into the public domain on Shabbat with weapons of war. It is clear that this would be permitted if required by security exigencies, but otherwise, one must avoid carrying weapons on Shabbat; that is the opinion of the sages. Yet Rabbi Eliezer permits it, and he offers a surprising rationale: just as a woman is permitted to go out on Shabbat wearing her jewels, which are considered accessories to her apparel, so, too, a man may go out arrayed in weapons because weapons are "his ornaments". How could one possibly consider weapons – which were designed for killing – an ornament? This idea is explained by Rav Kook in his commentary on this gemara[2]:

> **Heroism, in and of itself, is an ornament. Life's vigor in any form is good and proper; and external, bodily strength is ontologically linked to spiritual strength which is achieved only when the spirit is pure and honest. That is why those external signs – [like weapons] that indicate the existence of strength are also ornaments.**

---

1   **Mishnah**, *Shabbat* 6:4.
2   **Ein Aya**, Shabbat, chap. 6: 42. See an explanation of this issue in its entirety in **L'emunat Itenu**, IV pp. 93-119 [s.v. *"Bigvurot yesha yemino"*].

Physical power – for example, a person with strong muscles or one carrying weapons – while nothing more than external, should not be seen as a flaw but rather as a positive attribute, because physical power includes within its definition the vigor of life that is naturally connected to a positive internal quality, which is the power of the spirit. External strength is positive when it accompanies spiritual strength, a strength which is based on the purity and honesty existing in Man's soul by his very nature.

These succinct statements are not enough to explain the heart of the matter: what is the nature of that spiritual strength that turns the accompanying physical strength – into an ornament?

B. Heroism which stems from honesty

Roi elaborates on this theme in his notebook:

> Rabbi Eliezer says: They are his ornaments. The ornament is an external manifestation of what is inside. The ability to persevere and the vigor of spiritual life are connected to the physical ability to persevere. And this ability is good when its source is upright and pure.

The ability to persevere is finest, then, when it is founded on the spirit's ability to persevere, an ability whose source is "upright and pure". We must understand the concept of 'upright' as used in this context in the broadest sense:

> 'Uprightness' doesn't mean just not to lie, in the usual sense as in our regular usage of the term, but rather the forefathers of our nation were called 'upright' - compassionate, shy, and charitable, having a generous eye, a humble spirit,

and a diffident soul. It was Bilam who called the forefathers ' upright'.

We see that the concept 'upright' is very broad and encompasses all of the good qualities which characterized the forefathers of the nation and which are the hallmarks of the People of Israel.[3]

These words that Roi wrote are based to a large extent on the introduction by the *'Netziv* of Volozhin' to the Book of Genesis. The *Netziv* – Rabbi Naftali Zvi Yehuda Berlin – was the greatest of the Roshei Yeshiva (those sages who headed yeshivas) some one hundred and fifty years ago. Roi very much enjoyed his commentary on the Torah and used to study it at length. During all of the years that I studied with Roi, he would keep this commentary handy, and he frequently showed me the gems that he had discovered there. This is what the *Netziv* writes in his introduction to the Book of Genesis:

> **This book is called the Book of Genesis (*Breishit*); the prophets called it *Sefer Hayashar (literally "the Upright Book"),* as in the tractate of *Avoda Zara* (25a) when commenting on two verses from the Tanach: in the book of Joshua: "Is this not written in *Sefer Hayashar*?" (Josh. 10:13) and in the Book of Samuel: "To teach the children of Judah the use of the bow; behold, it is written in *Sefer Hayashar* (II Sam. 1:18). Rabbi Yohanan explains: This is the book of Abraham, Isaac, and Jacob who were called upright, as it is written: "Let me die the death of the upright" (Num. 23:10).**

The book recounting the deeds of the forefathers of the nation is called *Sefer Hayashar*, because our forefathers were called upright – *yashar*, to the point where in a moment of exalted enlightenment,

---

3 Based on **Talmud Bavli**, *Yevamot* 79a.

Bil'am wished that he might merit to be like these upright people. For example, our forefather Abraham was a paragon of compassion and benevolence; so great was his desire to act benevolently with every living creature that not only did he not rejoice when G-d announced his intention to destroy Sodom, but he went so far as to pray for the rescue of that city. This uprightness of our forefathers has persisted within us throughout the generations, in each generation according to its role.

The source of true heroism is in man's uprightness, from which power he draws the strength necessary to improve his own spiritual qualities, to act charitably, to have a generous eye and a humble spirit.

Here Roi adds in parentheses:

> 'Yashar' - which in Hebrew also means 'straight' - is the shortest distance between two points, and [a straight line] is also infinite, in the world of geometry. Uprightness - straightness - in the Torah is the source of positive characteristics such as mercy, etc.

Straightness is essentially the connection between many points, and in the area of the personality, it is the ability to weave together, with one line, noble spiritual qualities and to do this **consistently,** even in changing and complex situations. In light of this perception, it is appropriate to say that the honest person is, in effect, a **whole** person. And just as a straight line in geometry is infinite, so too in the spiritual world, the straight, upright person has an infinite desire to progress and without let-up, he makes higher and higher demands of himself; the straight, upright person consistently raises the bar of moral demands he places on himself.

C. Heroism in war as an act of benevolence

In light of this definition of uprightness as the qualities of
compassion and of unlimited benevolence in their perfect form, one
must investigate how uprightness is capable also of tying together
all of life's forces to the point of connecting qualities that seem
conflicting, such as benevolence to all and the ability to persevere
against all opposition:

> *The heroism displayed in war is an act of kindness
> so great that all other acts of kindness seem to
> vanish in comparison.*

Behind the scenes of the physical strength required on the battlefields
of Israel's wars is a great uprightnesss and a powerful aspiration
toward kindness that are embodied in one's deliberately putting
himself in a situation of danger in order to defend the nation.

This understanding of the attribute of *gevura* corresponds
to the one appearing in Rav Kook's commentary on the blessing
[recited each morning]: '*Ozer Yisrael b'gevura*' [Who girds Israel
with strength][4]:

> **The *gevura* of Israel is a special kind of *gevura*, a
> *gevura* that is distinguished not by conquests that
> suppress others, subdues them, or destroys them, but
> *gevura* which is essentially connected to the conquest
> a person makes of himself, the *gevura* of his Divine
> soul, that noble spirit that subdues the animal nature
> of his physical body and his brutish, untamed appetites,
> the *gevura* of someone who acts with forebearance is
> superior to the military hero and of he who masters his
> passions who is greater than the conqueror of a city.**

Someone who does not allow his anger to control him, a person

---

4   **Olat Reiyah**, I, p. 75.

who is self-restrained and in control of his behavior – is a greater hero than those who are generally considered heroes; the person who is master of his own passions and does not allow them to burst out irresponsibly – is a greater hero than the person who has succeeded in conquering a city.

> **That is the *gevura* with which Israel is girded, one appropriate to the principle of virtuous morality and to lifting Man in his preeminence over the beast.**

Gevura, then, is the ability to establish as dominant that element in ourselves that is upright and noble, that element of goodness and benevolence, and to have it control all the other life forces. Having clarified these points, our understanding of Rabbi Eliezer's words becomes deeper: In a person who is truly strong, a person of honesty and spiritual purity – his military strength is nothing less than testament to the nobility of his soul, the profundity of the unlimited benevolence that lies at the basis of his heroism in war.

D. Heroism is tested during periods of transition

Perhaps the most important situation in which a person's spiritual heroism is tested is a situation of transition. Frequently we have very fine wishes, ambitions that tug at our hearts and challenges that fire our imagination, but it is difficult to translate all of these into the reality of daily life, with all of its demands and the shifting states of mind that characterize it. A person who succeeds in living his life in "the real world" according to his profoundest moral demands is called upright, as if a straight line extends throughout his character from one end to the other, connecting all of the points in it to one objective; from the Jewish perspective, such a person is a hero.

The prayer '*Ana Bekoah*' is customarily recited at various times:

as part of *Kabbalat Shabbat,* before bed, after *Sefirat Haomer**, while reading, at the beginning of the *Shaharit* (morning) prayers, the *Korbanot* (verses and Talmudic sources describing the daily sacrifices), and in certain communities, even during a funeral. The common denominator of all of these times is that they are times of transition: transition between the weekday and the holiness of *Shabbat,* the transition between wakefulness and sleep, between Passover and *Shavuot,* the transition between this world and the next; these are highly-charged times that present a challenge to our moral status[5]. For example, the days of *Sefirat HaOmer,* days which originally had been a joyful period of spiritual uplifting between the exodus from Egypt and the giving of the Torah, are interspersed with days of mourning over the death of Rabbi Akiva's pupils. It seems that precisely because these days are charged with tremendous spiritual potential, they present us with the greatest demands, at a time when failure to meet them arouses against us the Divine attribute of unmitigated and exacting Justice[6].

E. Rabbi Nehunya ben Hakanah

The prayer *'Ana Be'koah'* is attributed to the sage Rabbi Nehunya ben Hakanah who also composed the prayers recited upon entering the bet midrash and upon leaving it, which are also points of transition. Rabbi Nehunya ben Hakanah seems to be an 'expert' in transitional moments. Rav Kook introduces his commentary on the prayer itself with a short discussion of the personality of Rabbi Nehunya ben Hakanah and the connection between it and the prayer:

---

5   See **Ein Aya**, chap. IV: par. 53, in the commentary on *tefillat haderech* (the Traveler's Prayer).

6   See **Kodesh ve-Hol**, p. 224.

* Counting the days between Passover and Shavuout in preparation for the day commemorating the giving of the Torah.

> Rabbi Nehunya ben Hakanah, upon entering the beit
> midrash and upon leaving it, would recite a brief
> prayer (tractate *Brachot* 28b), that he might safeguard
> all of the purity inherent in that which is holy, lest
> it be tainted through a possible deterioration caused
> by being in human society, even the holy and pure
> fellowship of Torah scholars who frequent the bet
> midrash. Rabbi Nehunya ben Hakanah, the man who
> rejoiced and delighted in his lot and knew that the
> corporeal, practical world was inferior and base, and
> that its only value in reality and existence is due to
> the light of Torah which is the life-spirit of the entire
> universe, this same Rabbi Nehunya ben Hakanah is
> the one who prayed to raise up all that was debased
> within existence, within the corporeal world of action,
> to the highest pinnacle, to spirituality, to the essence
> of the Torah and its exalted holiness.

Man's encounter with society is complex[7], liable to cause him to
deviate from his plans and virtuous intentions, out of a desire to win
the approval of others, or alternately, out of a desire to dominate
others. Even within the best society – the fellowship of scholars in
the beit midrash – the encounter with society is liable to taint the
human being. Rabbi Nehunya ben Hakanah is not oblivious to this:
he is conscious of these difficulties and composed a special prayer
to overcome them. We would expect that his prayer upon entering
the beit midrash would include a request for help from the Master
of the Universe in studying Torah, in the ability to maintain his
concentration and innovate ideas, but that is not the case; Rabbi
Nehunya ben Hakanah instead asks: "...that I may not fail in any
matter of halacha and that my fellows may rejoice in me...and that

---

7   See e.g. **Ein Aya**, Shabbat, chap. 1, par. 21: "...and as any man usually knows his
fellowman by his external side only, not his innermost nature, that is why society
may instill in itself sins born of habit and custom, things that were man to be allowed
to act naturally, he would never have come to commit those sins...".

my fellows not fail in any matter of halacha and that I may rejoice
in them..." He does not gloss over the complexity of the encounter
between people in all walks of life, including in the beit midrash,
but instead strives to cope with it successfully and not to fall. In
exiting the bet midrash he again urges us not to ignore the fact that
the world outside the beit midrash is not an ideal world, but one
that also includes "loafers and idle talk"[8] against which a person
must reinforce himself by rejoicing in the choice to follow the path
of Torah. Rabbi Nehunya ben Hakanah's prayers reflect a great
heroism expressed in their confrontation with the complexity of
reality, for the purpose of attaining complete mastery over all the
various aspects of life. This is the personality that also created the
prayer 'Ana Bekoah', from which we will try to learn and understand
several expressions.

The prayer 'Ana Bekoah' has a special structure. It has forty-
two words – a special number in itself: there is a special name of
G-d that has forty-two letters[9], in the first section of the *Shema*
there are forty-two words, and the Children of Israel went through
forty-two journeys in the desert[10]. The prayer is divided precisely
into seven sentences of six lines each. In certain sources it is stated
that the number forty-two signifies the moment the Divine will
chose to create the world, to turn ideas into reality[11], something
that connects very closely to everything that we have learned about
Rabbi Nehunya ben Hakanah. Although the prayer deals with what
is hidden in the deepest recesses of the soul of the Jewish collective,

---

8 Based on the prayer of Rabbi Nehunya ben Hakanah upon leaving the beit
midrash.
9 "Rabbi Judah said in the name of Rav: G-d's name that is comprised of forty-
two letters, one is not allowed to communicate it to a person who is not modest,
humble, and in the second half of life, a person who does not get angry, and does not
become intoxicated, and is forbearing. And anyone who knows it and is watchful of
it and guards it in purity is beloved above and agreeable below, and he is feared by
man, and inherits two worlds, this world and the world to come." **Talmud Bavli,**
Kiddushin 71a.
10 See **Rashi,** Num. 33:1.
11 See **Talmud Bavli,** *Hagiga* 11b, Tosefot s.v. "Ein dorshin".

we will nonetheless try to learn from it several things that pertain to the heroism of the individual.

F. "The joyful song of Your people"

The sentence "Accept the joyful song (*rina*) of Your nation, uplift us, purify us, O Awesome One" is interpreted by Rav Kook to mean:

> **When through the jubilation of joyous song (rina) – "*renana on the outside*" (Zohar) – the vital life forces awaken, impure, imperfect forces can accompany them and be awakened with them.**

Rav Kook explains that the joyful song expresses the external life forces which, by nature, are jubilant and spontaneous; the word *rinun* – like the word *rina* – is used to describe a rumor that circulates about on the outside. "Accept the joyful song of your people" – Be reconciled by the life forces bursting forth from Your people Israel. However, one must remember that when one turns outward, in spontaneous enthusiasm, the less positive forces in man may also awaken. Apart from the fact itself that crude, materialistic forces are aroused, the act of turning outward may cause a person to fall into superficiality, into a lack of fidelity to who he really is and to what he believes in. Rabbi Nehunya ben Hakanah, true to his personality, is not oblivious to these moral dangers, to the complexity involved in arousing external life forces.

> **For this we need the attribute of awe in its highest sense which sets limits on these forces and purifies the spirit of all dross, and the quality of *gevura* in it adds a hidden internal courage, to add height and the *gevura* of splendor in the deepest recesses of every soul.**

Rabbi Neḥunya ben Hakanah prays for alertness and attentiveness that will ensure that the external forces that break forth do not exceed the limits of good taste; in his prayer for awe in the highest sense which knows how to limit and control the life forces lies a tremendous *gevura*. It is precisely when we ask the Master of the Universe to accept our prayer in joyful song, to accept the powerful life forces, we add a request also for spiritual elevation and purity so that we are not enveloped by the impurities, the negative elements, attached to these forces, so that our lives will be pure in all realms.

This entreaty is a brave prayer that was composed by an upright hero who recognizes life's complexity and wants to control and guide it.

G. "Those who remember your holiness"

In his commentary on the continuation of the prayer – "One and Only Exalted One, turn to your nation which remembers Your holiness", Rav Kook refers to the transitions and vicissitudes that the nation of Israel undergoes in the course of its history. He writes:

> **And despite all of the reversals that it [the Jewish nation] has experienced, despite all of the abysses into which it has plunged, despite all of the harshness of the limitations of the worlds of physical action and the raging, torrential storm-waves that cause all of the Divine splendor to be forgotten, it is these people who remember the Divine holiness, the holiness of the One, the One who is at the pinnacle of existence, whose loftiness is greater than the world can contain.**

There are complex and complicated situations – storm-waves –

when energies and impulses may cause the Divine splendor to be forgotten; the flow of life may cause us to forget something that we very much want and which we know. It is to counter this that the prayer "to remember the holiness" is directed. The person who remembers holiness is entitled to seek help from the Master of the Universe. When the Jewish people remembers that it has an internal code that it will never renounce for any wealth in the world, it is attuned to its inner voice and does not fall into the snare of forgetfulness. A person who adopts this quality in his personal life, a person to whom periods of transition and the raging torrents of the times do not cause him to forget – is a hero and as such, is entitled to help from above in order to strengthen the element of *gevura* in himself.

H. The entreaty and the cry

In the next line – "Accept our entreaty and hear our cry, O Knower of mysteries" – the expressions of powerful, almost desperate, intensity stand out: 'entreaty', 'cry'. Rav Kook comments on this:

> **How far does the intensity of Man's thirst for G-d in His purity reach, even to the highest point of Divine purification, and how far does his sorrow at confinement and languishing in the darkness reach? This is something that no living creature knows; only the Master of all, blessed be He, He who alone knows all mysteries, it is He who knows the intensity of the light regarding which, in proportion to the measure of a man's longing, his entreaty will intensify, and it is He knows the depth of the darkness in whose constraints the soul finds itself bound.**

Someone who wants to be a true hero places himself, consciously, into a reality that is far from simple. It is that person who believes wholeheartedly in his ability to adhere to his spiritual principles even when they demand strength of will and effort, who will also have very high expectations of himself, expectations that come from a heightened spiritual sensibility. It is easy for such a person to fall into despair that comes from a sense of not being able to meet the challenges that he has set for himself. No one can truly see the tremendous work that the hero does inwardly. It is only the Creator of the world – the Knower of mysteries – who can appreciate the hero's efforts to control his own life, to be aware of himself, to be alert in regard to all of his life-forces, and to constrain them when necessary. We cry out for help from the Knower of mysteries, help that will manifest itself by giving us the strength necessary to be heroes, because only He knows how much help we need to truly succeed at this.

I. The heroism of perseverance

The attribute of *gevura* is capable of bringing a person to a situation where he can "sign off" on every piece of his life: every minute detail, every single deed, and every last response. He can say: "Yes, I was there with full moral cognizance, that is how I wanted to respond, that corresponds to my world of values". The hero has no unit of time in his life when he fails by forgetting uprightness and abandoning his values. When this kind of heroism, the heroism of uprightness and nobility, goes to war, this is a heroism that is full of unbounded giving, heroism that is the opposite of impulsivity, and this was the kind of hero that Rabbi Eliezer envisioned when he ruled that the sword and the bow are also ornaments.

In the passage previously quoted, the *Netziv* referred to the verse: "To teach the children of Judah the use of the bow; behold, it is written in the Book of Yashar". The person who wants to teach the children of Judah how to use the bow must know the character of the human beings entrusted with using all of our weapons systems: what uprightness, what heroism of spirit are stored in these Jewish souls.

It came to me that one may explain through this approach the concept that the sages use to describe the falling of rain – *gevurat geshamim*[12] [=the power of the rains] or as Rabbi Yohanan said, "The rain falls with *gevura*". When water descends from the skies, it does not fall in undifferentiated torrents but in drops. The falling of the rain in just this manner and not as a flood that could engulf us is a tremendous kindness that the Holy One, blessed be He, does for us. He brings us the tremendous power of the rains in measured quantities that we are able to absorb, an enormous quantity of water that appears in an incalculable number of drops. Perhaps this can serve as a parable as to how the quality of *gevura* should be manifested in Man: the hero is someone who is capable of separating all of his personal powers and energies into precise, measured drops, through considered actions and deliberate responses. The power of such a personality is revealed very gradually, and its true test comes in times of transition.

For example, the first sentence in the *Shulhan Aruch* states: "Display the *gevura* of a lion to arise in the morning to serve the Creator". When a person gets up in the morning, he calls upon the attribute of *gevura* because when he went to sleep he might have made all kinds of plans for the morning, but now when he begins to stir, all of his grand plans must be channeled into one point of volition, that is, the decision at that moment to get out of bed.

---

12 **Talmud Bavli,** *Ta'anit* 2a.

J. Roi's heroism

It is not easy for me to end our study of this subject. As more time passes, the feelings of wistful longing for Roi only grow stronger. I don't know who said that time heals; I feel that the opposite is true. There is so much to miss, but in the context of *gevura* as we have just learned about it, the feelings of loss arise for the quality of every particular and detail in Roi's life. These are not feelings of loss only for a beloved person but for a rare occurrence, a genuine phenomenon. Roi set for himself standards of *gevura* that always left me standing in awe. Total control, a conscious decision about each and every moment, each deed, each word, every response. Beyond my regretful longings for Roi as a friend, they are for the loss to this world of *middot* (character traits) that are very nearly incomparable.

Already in our first encounter, in the first gemara lesson, when I was in the role of the teacher and he was in the role of pupil, I made a mental note to myself that on that day I had met a pupil who was a hero. We did not yet knew each other, we had not yet spoken together, but time sharpens an educator's sensibilities about pupils, and I saw before me a pupil who had made a conscious decision that he would not allow himself even one second in the lesson to be unfocused; he had taken upon himself to be present with every element of his personality at any given moment in the lesson. We cannot take this commitment of his lightly, because it is a very rare occurrence. Even in people who have a strong will and ability, there are waves of concentration and attentiveness, ups and downs, better and worse moments, and the ability to remove oneself from this natural human weakness could only come on the heels of a very resolute decision. Throughout, he demonstrated a powerful commitment to the attribute of *gevura*. Notions such as "I'm tired"; "I don't have any more strength", and "Maybe today we'll study a little less", were not part of his lexicon. And so it continued, every day, and all of the hours that make up the day, and all of the moments that make up the hours. Incalculable moments of decision – to realize potential, to "sign off" on every single minute, every single response.

In reference to the prayer that is recited upon entering the beit midrash, we mentioned that the beit midrash is also a place where there are social relationships; when two people study together, a certain veiled tension is liable develop between them – Who is taking the lead in study? Who has more new ideas? In studying with Roi there was none of that: everything was so concentrated, deliberate, and principled, that there was no chance that such a thing would develop. In this sense, we were privileged to study together in a very pure style.

Perhaps we may alleviate our great pain with a humorous story that is relevant to our subject: after the screening of the film in memory of Roi, Dudi Zilbershlag[13] said that until he saw the film – he did not know that Roi used to get up early in the morning to study. He added that he also does this; he wakes up early and studies at the *Kotel*. Here, with a smile, he added in the name of the Baal Shem Tov* that in the early hours of the morning – the hours that one needs *gevura* in order to wake up – the air in the world is the purest because the revelers of the previous night have already gone to bed while the swindlers of the morning have not yet woken up...

---

13 Head of the charitable organization 'Koah La'tet', about which Roi did his final project for his degree in industrial engineering and management, together with his friend Benny Kuperman. See later in the book, in chapter 9.

* Rabbi Yisrael Baal Shem Tov (1698-1760), founder of the Hassidic movement.

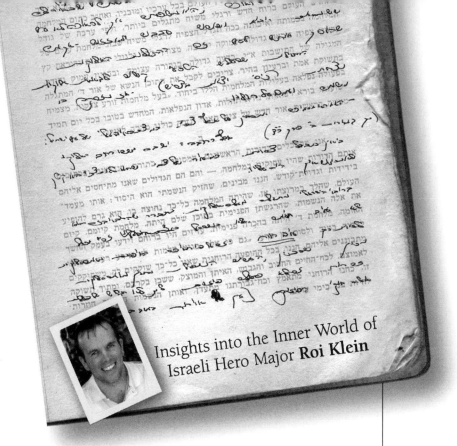

Insights into the Inner World of
Israeli Hero Major **Roi Klein**

Chapter 7

In awe of Heaven

In awe of Heaven

A. The purpose of Torah study

We are now a short time after *Shavuot* and after the *hachnasat* Sefer Torah written in Roi's memory, which is an appropriate time to elucidate that fundamental element of psyche and character that is at the basis of our connection with the Torah.

For two years a small group, among them Roi, would get together twice a week and discuss the Maharal's work '*Tiferet Yisrael*'. The book has seventy chapters and its main theme is the receiving of the Torah. Every week all of the participants would prepare a chapter or two in independent study, and then we would meet to discuss the main themes of each chapter and summarize the ideas; the memory of the festive *siyum*[**]of this book is clearly etched in my mind.

---

[*] Translator's Note: *Yirat shamayim*, awe of G-d who is beyond and above us, is defined variously as fear of G-d, piety, and reverence. Because the author's definition contrasts it with fear, I have left it in the Hebrew where appropriate.

[**] festive completion ceremony of a tractate or religious book.

Roi left behind a notebook in which he would summarize this study and in his summary of chapter 10, whose subject is the connection between Torah study and *yirat shamayim*, he wrote a succinct sentence which we will use to get into the subject:

The purpose of studying the Talmud is to shape a person's personality...to build a life that is filled with humanity and spiritual content, and not just intellectual ideas.

The subject we are addressing here is a clarification of the purpose of that study which Roi placed at the center of his scholarly endeavor – the study of Talmud. This study is not meant to merely add something to a person's store of knowledge but to introduce him to the way the Torah looks at different situations that are characteristic of the human condition as it really is and at a range of different subjects that are included in the course of a life. The *Mishnah*, the book on which the *Gemara* is based, is comprised of six sections, or *sedarim* (orders): the order of *Zera'im* deals with the relationship between man and the land, and everything connected to agriculture according to the Torah; the order of *Moed* clarifies the issue of time; the order of *Nashim* deals with family life; the order of *Nezikin* deals with legal justice. Over the generations, rabbinical scholars have deliberated and debated issues included in the contents of these orders, as well as the others: *Kodashim* ("Holy things" regarding sacrifices, the Temple, and the dietary laws), and *Taharot*, "Purities", pertaining to the laws of purity and impurity) and the purpose of all of these deliberations is to shape the personality of the learner and to develop his spiritual life. In his notebook Roi emphasized the word '**life**' and for very good reason: the emphasis is on real life and not just on theories. That kind of study whose purpose is attaining a life of holiness we call study born of *yirat shamayim* for the sake of *yirat shamayim*.

Many places, both in the Tanach and in the words of the sages, emphasize that the purpose of Torah study is to acquire *yirat shamayim.* In the book of Psalms it is written: "The beginning of wisdom is fear of God",[1] the beginning of **all** wisdom is *yirat shamayim*; and in the end of the book of *Kohelet* (Ecclesiastes), King Solomon, the wisest of all men, says: "The end of the matter when all is said and done: Fear G-d and keep His commandments for that is the whole of man".[2] Before the *musaf* service on a Shabbat when we say the blessing for the new month, we ask the Master of the Universe for "a life in which we will have love of Torah and *yirat shamayim*"[3], because love of Torah is not enough by itself. Based on that same principle, the Talmud compares someone who studies Torah without working on his *yirat shamayim* to the person who gathers in his crop from the field and stores it but does not take pains to do the work necessary to preserve the grain[4]; the crop will rot within a short time, so that there is no purpose to the great amount of toil that went into harvesting and storing it. The purpose of study is, then, to shape a whole personality in the spirit of the Torah, a personality that is full of Torah and *yirat shamayim.*

B. Mistaken perceptions of 'fear of Heaven'

The term *'yirat shamayim'* is very charged, and one may err and understand it in a threatening way to the point of even developing an aversion to it. Rav Kook has this to say about the term[5]:

> The concept of *'yirat shamayim'* adds valor and strength to the soul of the man who understands it in its purity, it causes life to be full of interest and great

---

1   **Psalms** 111:10.
2   **Kohelet** 12:13.
3   From the prayer composed by Rav (**Mishnah**, *Brachot* 16:1) said on the Shabbat before the new month begins.
4   **Mishnah**, *Shabbat*, 31:1.
5   **Midot Ha-Reiya,** chapter on *Yirah*, 3, [p. 76].

aspirations, and fills it with sublime spirituality that purifies the abilities of the psyche with the light of a holy fire. However, for the foolish it presents itself as a symbol of terror that causes weakness, despair, and helplessness.

A terrified person is a weak person, one who cannot find within himself the emotional strength to take any meaningful action, and therefore:

This influence is very harmful, and when it spreads it causes a rebellion against the entire concept of the 'yoke of the kingdom of heaven' in the young people who have had a taste of a full-bodied life, who rightly wish for a life free of dread and terror, a life filled instead with valor and the assurance of courage.

That is why we must understand as correctly as possible the term 'yirat shamayim' and to differentiate resolutely between it and the term 'fear' [פחד]. Perhaps the major error in understanding the concept of 'yirah' in the world of the holy is the idea that we are speaking of fear in the usual psychological sense[6]. A person who is afraid is a shrunken person – physically and psychologically; it is hard for him to think straight and to act, he lacks the power to be a leader or a hero. All that he wants is to get through the day without anything bad happening to him. He does not initiate and he is not alert – he is closed. The Holy One, blessed be He, did not give us Torah in a divine revelation from heaven in order to produce people who are frightened and closed![7] An illustration of the fact that yirah (awe) is not fear is the commandment to have yirah for one's parents; when the Torah commands us to show yirah in relation

---

6   Editor's note: Nonetheless Rav Kook did write in several places that Man also needs a certain measure of 'fear of punishment' for those parts of the human psyche that are not sufficiently illuminated by the light of pure yirat Hashem. See extensive discussions of this in **Orot Hakodesh**, IV, 413-433.

7   See the article on fear in Rav Kook, **Ikvei Hatzon**, 119-121.

to our parents – "Every man shall have reverence for his mother and father"[8] – this does not mean that children should walk about their homes in terror, hugging the walls, in fear and apprehension of what their parents might do to them... Normal parents do not want their children to relate to them this way, so to have *yirah* of parents does not mean to be in fear of them.

Furthermore, *yirat shamayim* is not **obedience**. Like fear, blind obedience is not a great virtue. Can a society of obedient pawns – whether they are that way out of fear or because of brainwashing – be full of life, interest, aspirations and talents, as described by Rav Kook?

Therefore we must take apart the two words that make up the term '*yirat shamayim*' to understand each separately: what is '*yirah*' and what is '*shamayim*', and as a result of that, we can understand what is '*yirat shamayim*'.

C. The atmosphere in the house of the king

In his notebook on the same page, Roi wrote a succinct definition for the term '*yirat shamayim*':

> Yirat Shamayim - subordinating ourselves to the heavenly content that expresses itself within us (and not something that is foreign to us).

This definition is a unique one of the concept of *yirat shamayim* as subordinating oneself, in other words, the recognition and the understanding that there is something primary and something that is secondary to it, and that which is secondary knows to diminish its own importance when facing that which is primary.

---

8   **Lev.** 19:3.

Afterwards Roi adds a rather enigmatic sentence:

To live a life of loyalty to the kingdom, one that revolves around the King's daughter, who lives within us.

Who is "the King's daughter who lives within us"? And what is the "life of loyalty to the kingdom" that we must live? The key to unraveling this sentence is found in a well-known *midrash* about the soul of Man[9]:

> **To what is this analogous? To the case of a burgher who married a princess. If he brought her all that the world possessed, it would mean nothing to her. Why? Because of her being a king's daughter. So is it with the soul. If you were to bring the soul all the delights of the world, they would be as nothing to it. Why? Because it belongs to a higher, transcendent existence.**

The soul of Man is compared to a king's daughter, and in order to delve into the deeper meaning of this parable, we must try to think like the king's daughter. According to this analogy, there is a gaping abyss between the nature of the life of the typical citizen and that of the king and his family. While the world of the man in the street revolves around his personal success, and perhaps that of his close family, the life of someone who dwells in the royal palace is a different life, one that revolves around the state and the kingdom. Unlike the family of the prosperous citizen where they listen to the news once a day if at all, in the house of the king's daughter, they are preoccupied all day with the burning issues of the kingdom, from an incalculable number of aspects and angles. She grew up in a house where phrases such as "It's not my business" or "I'm busy now with my own affairs" do not exist, because the king is called upon at all times to provide solutions and answers to all of the problems of the kingdom. If anyone would try to engage the king's daughter with

9 Ecc. Rabba, VI, 7.

issues that are purely personal, she would object, because all of her life she has been absorbing the royal atmosphere, concern for that which is universal rather than personal.

The purpose behind this *midrash* is to call our attention to the fact that in our soul there is a kingly element; the source of the soul is in the king's palace. For the time being it is here, within the limitations and constraints of the body to which it is "wed", but as for itself, it will always be incomparably broader and greater than the body. We have within us aspirations, values, conscience, and a natural interest in what is beyond the small private domain of the individual. We have in the kernel of our personality a very broad and universalistic fundamental element; we have within us "a king's daughter". The king's daughter demands that we live a life of commitment to the kingdom as a whole, that is, a life in which we do not think only of ourselves. Hers is an unending demand that we think about our fellowman, that we expand and deepen our knowledge, that we be concerned about society and about all of mankind. Our soul calls upon us unceasingly: Don't limit your world to only your own life, expand your perspective! Don't close yourself off, don't shrink inward, open yourself to the Divine greatness that flows throughout all of existence!

The everyday citizen, who all his life has lived an ordinary life, finds it hard to understand the king's daughter to whom he is wed, he tries to force-feed her with the limited materials that he is familiar with and thinks, mistakenly, that if he would only increase the quantity of this material, the king's daughter would be satisfied; however, her need is one that cannot be quieted. It will continue to spur her husband to strive constantly for greater heights.

D. The heavenliness within us

This understanding of the soul that we have within us gives us access to a better understanding of the concept of *'shamayim'*[heaven] and thus to understanding the term *'yirat shamayim'.* What do we mean when we say 'heaven' in the spiritual sense? When a person looks at the earth, the range of his vision is very limited, because of the mountains, hills, and contours of the variable landscape; however, when we lift our eyes to the heavens, we can see vast expanses that cannot be encompassed. This heavenliness, then, is the opposite of narrow horizons and small-mindedness. **Yirat shamayim – awe of the G-d above us – requires us to subordinate ourselves to the heavenliness that expresses itself within us.**[10] We have within ourselves something of the heavens, we have within us an element that expands our thinking and our psyche and we should subordinate ourselves to this element of our identity. The private, limited house must know how to make itself secondary to the royal palace; physicality and narrow existentiality, being grounded in time and space, should defer to spirituality and universality. For if we were to meet a genuine king, e.g. of the nature of King David, who is involved only in matters of state and the general welfare, the minute that we began to talk to him about our private problems – we would be filled with feelings of shame. To waste the time of a person who is totally preoccupied with the needs of the collective for trivial matters?! A narrow vision subordinates itself to the infinite expanse, the earth diminishes its own importance before the heavens. *Yirat shamayim* is setting aside

---

10 Editor's note: The idea in this chapter of the centrality of Man's Divine soul as being so great that a man should subordinate himself to it, is based on the straightforward understanding that the soul is Man's bridge, so to speak, to the King Himself (Hashem), to He who transcends all definition, and about whom it is written: "the heaven and heaven of heavens cannot contain You" (I Kings 8:27). Plainly, without a king there can be no "king's daughter". Therefore when we speak of subordinating ourselves to the "king's daughter who is within us", this is only because we have subordinated ourselves to the king himself, a subordination of the limited and the finite to He who is beyond all definition. See **Ma'amrei Ha-Reiya,** p.507.

the minor things in life in the face of the truly great ones which exist in the innermost depths of every person. *Yirat shamayim* does not come from something foreign but rather from within. It is not fear of something alien, nor is it blind obedience, but rather, it is an internal, honest decision **to subordinate ourselves to Hashem, whose heavenliness is expressed within ourselves.**

E. Torah, divinely revealed from Heaven

This insight, that "heaven" is a parable referring to the Divine source of the highest internal content that is hidden deep within us ["heavenliness"], has a number of ramifications. One of them is the undeniable necessity of "Torah from Heaven". In another place in his book '*Tiferet Yisrael*', the *Maharal* says of the king's daughter who was wed to an ordinary citizen[11]:

> **And this necessitates that Torah must be a revelation from Heaven, for those who know the essence of the soul and its spiritual level, that the soul is from Heaven, and that it is an incomplete being and therefore its completion is through the Torah and the commandments.**

The structure of our soul requires that we have a Divinely-revealed Torah, that must come from Heaven and no other, more mundane, source. The soul must be addressed in the language that is natural to it, the language of royalty, for the language of the mundane citizen does not satisfy it. In the verses that describe the giving of the Torah, it is emphasized: "You have seen that I have spoken with you **from the heavens**"[12]. It is obvious that we cannot even hypothesize what the Children of Israel absorbed at the revelation

---

11 **Tiferet Yisrael**, end of chapter 4.
12 **Ex.** 20:18.

at Sinai, but at least in the external description of the event, one can see that throughout the revelation at Sinai those who are present are looking at the heavens, where a cloud and lighting appear; the motif of the giving of the Torah is the heavens, the infinite expanses that are revealed within the Torah. *Yirat shamayim* includes opening oneself up to the greatness that is hidden within ourselves; therefore, it is clear how it adds vigor and strength to the soul of Man, and transforms life into something that is full of interest and great aspirations[13].

If, nonetheless, there is a certain measure of real fear expressed in the term *yirat shamayim* in its purity, then it must be the fear of remaining small, lacking in greatness, lacking in expansive horizons and broad responsibility, which goes beyond the responsibility that everyone has for his own private sphere. Smallness of mind and spirit, narrow horizons, an inability to love, to grow, and to learn – these are truly to be feared.

Another ramification of this insight is that **heavenliness is already within us.** We can and must accept the fact of the Divine revelation of the Torah because it corresponds to the content that was established within us even before the giving of the Torah. Even within a Jew who does not study Torah, and does not observe the *mitzvot*, there is a measure of *yirat shamayim*, whether he wants it or not. In the very ability to distinguish between a petty thing and a great one, between what is noble and what is base, there is a measure of *yirat shamayim*. Every person who is able to set his priorities based on a value-oriented perspective, who is capable of setting aside his individuality in favor of universality – has some measure of *yirat shamayim*.

---

13 Based on the words of Rav Kook quoted above, no. 5.

F. Natural ethical behavior is the basis of Torah

It may be that it is that nuclear *yirat shamayim* – that innate quality of Man connecting him to greatness, which is the only pure foundation for accepting the yoke of Torah and mitzvot – to which the sages referred when they said that *"Derech Eretz* kadma leTorah"* – Derech Eretz comes before Torah[14], namely *derech eretz* as the natural form of *yirat shamayim* which each and everyone of us has inside of him, even before everything that he acquired through Torah study. It is from there that there is a will to be "heavenly", not in the sense of being a person whose head is in the clouds but rather a person with broad horizons and an aspiration to greatness.

Rav Kook writes about this in 'Orot Ha-Torah'[15]:

> **Derech Eretz must always precede Torah; morality in its most natural state, in the full depth of its splendor and robust power must be firmly fixed in the soul and be the basis for those great influences that come by virtue of the Torah. And just as *yirah* acts as the root that precedes wisdom, so is natural morality like the root that precedes *yirah* and all of its offshoots.**

The spiritual infrastructure for Torah and *Yirah* is natural morality which is also, in effect, *yirat shamayim*. "If there is no fear of God, there is no wisdom"[16]; "Anyone whose fear of sin takes priority over his wisdom, his wisdom will endure; but anyone whose wisdom takes priority over his fear of sin, his wisdom will

---

14 **Tana D'vei Eliyahu Rabba**, parsha 1; **Lev. Rabba** parsha 9, 3; See also **Mishnah,** *Avot* 3, 17.

15 **Orot Ha-Torah**, 12, 2.

16 **Mishnah,** *Avot*, 3, 17.

* Derech Eretz, natural ethical behavior, usually means both courteous and moral interpersonal behavior, as well as being involved in developing the world

not endure"[17]. When a person identifies the king's daughter within himself, when he feels concern and responsibility – it is a sign that the Torah is speaking to him because he and the Torah speak the same language.

The quality of *yirat shamayim* is determined by the degree of alertness that a person shows for the Divine image within himself. A person's *yirat shamayim* expresses itself in those decisions he makes throughout life in which he preferred the general over the personal, expansiveness over narrowness. Any demonstration of preference for greatness over smallness has an aspect of *yirat shamayim*. *Yirat shamayim* is a dynamic, continual occurrence, every hour and every minute, it is a developing state of the soul.

G. To always be in awe of Heaven

In Tana D'vei Eliyahu there is a special definition of *yirat shamayim* that we recite every morning in our prayers: "One should always be in awe of Heaven"[18]. Rav Kook says about this[19]:

> **The essence of Man is *yirat shamayim*, full *yirat shamayim*, one that pervades his inner being and that has a strong, vital influence to the point where the nature of its influence is noticeable in all of life's endeavors. "Fear G-d and keep His commandments for that is the whole of man". And Man must not at any time, at any minute of his life be deprived of his essential nature which is *yirat shamayim* in its complete form.**

Yirat shamayim is the full realization of being human. It is Man's

---

17 *Avot,* 3, 9.
18 **Eliyahu Rabba,** parsha 18 s.v. *"l'olam yehe adam".*
19 **Olat Reiyah**, I, p.101.

loyalty to the image of G-d that is in him, **it is the essence of Man,** and it is always proper for Man to be *yerei shamayim*, to be **Man** at all times.

In light of what we have learned up to now, we can understand why *yirat shamayim* is the essence of Man, and because it is the essence of Man, he should aspire to it every moment, at all times, unceasingly.

When Rav Kook first arrived in the Land of Israel, he served as the rabbi of Jaffa and the surrounding settlements. Jaffa was a very important city at that time, the only city in the Sharon and coastal region, and all of the settlements at that time – such as Rehovot, Ness Ziona, and Gedera – were concentrated around it. Jerusalem was full of rabbis, among them Rabbi Yaakov Moshe Harlap, who used to travel regularly to Jaffa in order to learn Torah first-hand from Rav Kook. When he was asked why he saw fit to attach himself in this way to Rav Kook, when Jerusalem had an abundance of great rabbis and *tzaddikim*, he answered that he knew great Torah scholars who were great most hours of the day, but they also had some hours when they were like everyone else; but not Rav Kook, who never had any hours of smallness. He was great twenty-four hours a day[20]. He was a man who was never without *yirat shamayim* for even one minute of his life.

H. Above all else – Yirat shamayim

We are called upon at every moment to decide anew who we are and to expand our receptiveness to greatness and universality, and this demand is not easy. The path of a person who is in awe of the Heavens is paved with internal struggles and conflicts. In his book about attributes of character (*midot*), Rav Kook describes the

20 Quoted in **Likutei Ha-Reiyah**, p. 413.

classical struggle of the person who is in awe of the Heavens[21]:

The spirit of the brave man who knows by virtue of his inner essence that this feeling of fear of G-d is all – all of life and all of that which is good – will not abandon his treasure. Through whatever suffering he undergoes, physical torments and spiritual torments, through all that which it seems he will be unable to withstand as he confronts the freedom of modernity, the great cultural aspiration of temporal life, the alluring beauty and the tumultuous perception of life, and sometimes even natural morality and honesty, which he is not always able to accommodate to fit the mold of fear of G-d and its real-life ramifications as he explains these to himself – all of these will not possess the power to sever the thread of life and the strength of the conviction that only fear of G-d provides a powerful shelter for Man.

The subject described above is the concern over a sense of contradiction, as it were, that exists between *yirat shamayim* and other important things that exist in every person's life, such as the "freedom of modernity".

It seems that the truest of the principles that have appeared in the entire modern age, throughout the revolution that mankind has undergone in recent centuries, is the concept of 'freedom'. The concept of freedom contains within it a tremendous power that must be acknowledged; freedom as a value affects all areas of life in our times: science, culture, politics, family life, and more. One should not deny the value of human freedom, but one must know that there is something greater than it – *yirat shamayim*, Man's ability to "breathe rarified air" and to belong to the kingdom. If a person were presented with the choice between two options: to

---

21 **Midot Ha-Reiyah**, Yirat Hashem , p. 76.

do "what he feels like doing" or to help the Prime Minister or an important minister in a matter of top national importance, there is no doubt that a decent person would choose the second option and would even be very happy with his choice, despite the fact that he has given up his freedom to handle his own private affairs. He will be filled with a sense of belonging, and will feel that he is **Man** in the fullest sense of this word.

In a life where the value of freedom takes center stage, there is a lot of tumult, because everyone expresses himself with all of his might. We have no objection in principle to self-expression but one must understand that *yirat shamayim* is above that, too.

And that is how it is also in relation to "natural morality and honesty": the person who has *yirat shamayim* knows how to subordinate himself to the Divine greatness and knows that sometimes there is a clash between morality as portrayed by the human mind and Divine morality, which is more universal, more profound, and, therefore, decisive.

I. Roi's Yirat shamayim

We have discussed the subject of *yirat shamayim*, and have tried to acquaint ourselves with this concept in its purest form. When *yirat shamayim* is understood in this way, it becomes something that preoccupies a person at all times. Our first appeal every day to the Master of the universe is like an appeal to a king: "Modeh Ani – I thank you, living and eternal King" and the use of this term is precisely because the first thing for which we give thanks is the fact that we have within us the daughter of a king "for restoring **my soul** within me". We thank the King that he has given us the king's daughter, that he has planted in us an essence that is kingly, heavenly, and universal. Even before we have completely opened our eyes, and before we have begun to deal with our body, we immediately give thanks for the main thing: that we have within us the king's daughter. This is the headline that sets the tone for the rest of the day; this is a moment of *yirat shamayim*.

Yirat shamayim instills in a person a sense of serenity, because he knows with certainty that he belongs to something mighty, and this realization floods him with joy. In the prayers on Shabbat we say: "Those who observe the Shabbat will rejoice in your kingship" – the knowledge that we belong to the Kingship of Hashem is joyous knowledge, not frightening. The person who knows that his life has a broader significance feels satisfaction; the only fear that he has is the fear that he might be small, the fear that he might lose one day or even one hour in smallness and meaninglessness.

That was the inner world in which Roi lived. These few words about *yirat shamayim* which he put in parentheses "not something that is foreign to us" – are the essence of his personality as I knew it. Not to be superficial, not even for one minute.

In choosing to place *yirat shamayim* at the center of his aspirations, there was neither fear nor blind obedience, neither childish submission nor terror of what could happen to him; instead, it was a conscious and resolute decision, full of assurance and power, a decision full of purity whose concern was to live a life of the kingdom revolving around the king's daughter, and to accept the yoke of the kingdom of heaven with joy. The angels are described in the morning prayers as competing among themselves for the right to be the first to accept the yoke of heaven. We do not understand very much about the nature of angels, but we do know that they are described, both in the Tanach and in the rabbinic literature, as being among those who sing. Accepting the yoke of the kingdom of heaven, then, is song, it is a decision that life will not be gray and neutral, undefined, but rather full of greatness. And this is said not only of those who have a public task; a private home that has in it Torah and *hesed*, a household where thinking is from a general perspective – that discusses how to grow and how to make spiritual progress, a house where there is a preference to giving to one's fellowman over a preoccupation with oneself – is guaranteed to be a house full of joy and song.

That is the diligence in Torah study that I was privileged to be near, diligent Torah study that was aimed entirely at the innermost point, at *yirat shamayim*, at building a full life in the light of Hashem.

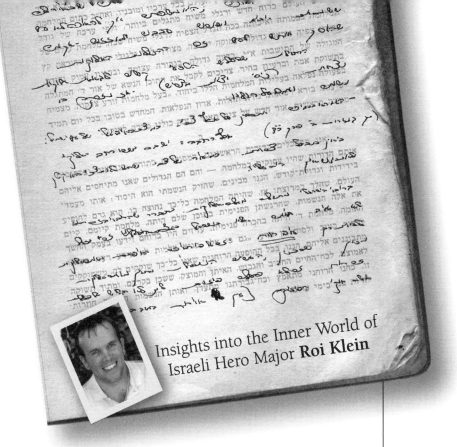

Insights into the Inner World of
Israeli Hero Major **Roi Klein**

Chapter 8

To Love the Land of Israel Purely

To Love the Land of Israel Purely

A. Eretz hatzvi (Land of the deer)

B. The rapid development of the Land of Israel

C. A good, broad, and expanding land

D. The land of peace

E. A pure economy

F. A pure army

G. The inner truth of the Land

H. The consolations of the Land of Israel

A. Eretz hatzvi (Land of the deer)

The common denominator of all of the meetings that we have held over the course of the year is our attempt to explore the character traits of Roi; however, beyond that there are several subjects that I think Roi would very happy that we are discussing, since they were so close to his heart. That is the way I feel about the subject that we are going to talk about tonight – our connection to the Land of Israel. In the film made in Roi's memory, Sarah recounted that she woke Roi up one night and told him that she was having trouble falling asleep. Roi answered her in his sleep: "Think about good things, think about the people of Israel, about the Land of Israel." And then after a moment of silence, he added in his sleep: "and about the connection between them..." In the morning he didn't remember a thing. This story attests to how much Roi lived our connection as a nation with this land. Because of the depth of the subject, it can be looked at from many angles, and we shall try to look at it from the angle that deals with the moral and spiritual meaning of our material development here in Israel.

In his book 'Netzah Yisrael' the Maharal of Prague discusses the subject of the exile and redemption and in this context he constructed a complete blueprint describing the Land of Israel as we would like it to be, the ideal Land of Israel. In several places in the Tanach, the Land of Israel is mentioned alongside the image of 'Hatzvi'[1] [=deer] and is also called 'Eretz Hatzvi'[2] in the Book of Daniel. We understand without difficulty the meaning of the more familiar names 'the Holy Land', 'the Promised Land' but less understood is the meaning of the name 'Eretz Hatzvi' (=the land of the deer). What is the connection between the deer – a species of animal – and the Land of Israel, and what message is supposed to be understood by calling the Land of Israel by this name 'Eretz Hatzvi'? We will look at two different explanations that appear in the gemara on this subject, and the in-depth explanation of the Maharal on them.

B. The rapid development of the Land of Israel.

The gemara in tractate Ketubot[3] says:

> **Why was the Land of Israel compared to a deer? Because just as the deer is swifter than all the other animals, so is the Land of Israel swifter than all the other lands to ripen its fruits.**

Just as the deer is swift-footed, so, too, when the people of Israel and the Land of Israel are united, the land gives forth its fruits quickly[4], and it seems to me that one may understand the word 'fruits' here as describing not only the land's agricultural produce but rather all

1   **Jer.** 3:19; **Ezek.** 20: 6, 15.

2   **Dan.** 11: 16, 41.

3   **Talmud Bavli**, Ketubot 112a.

4   Editor's note: Although from the words of the gemara by themselves, it would seem that the virtue of rapid growth belongs to the land itself, without any connection to the nation, nevertheless we have adopted the Maharal's interpretation quoted immediately afterward, and furthermore, this idea has much support in the sources, among others, sources dealing with this very subject in Ketubot.

of its development and growth in all fields. The contact between the land of Israel and the people of Israel brings about very rapid achievements, which are unconventional, and thank G-d that we have been privileged to see these things with our own eyes in the last generations.

Ostensibly the description given in the gemara is a material, economic depiction, but what is its spiritual meaning? Why is the gemara interested in the material theme that speaks of the proliferation of orchards and factories, settlements and roads in the Land of Israel? Why does it "bother" to compose such a lovely parable about the resemblance of the Land of Israel to a deer? We are forced to arrive at the realization that the material development of the Land of Israel has spiritual significance, and it was this subject that Roi loved to discuss.

The Maharal says about this[5]:

> **The Holy Land, when its [rightful] residents are living in it – which is fitting for the Land, and that is the vitality of the Land, because Hashem blessed be He gave the Land to the People of Israel, and it is called therefore the Land of Israel, therefore the vitality of the land exists specifically when its [rightful] residents – the People of Israel – are living in it. Then it has a transcendent excellence in all realms, [even] that it is swift to ripen its fruit, and that shows that it has an excellence that is non-material. Just as the deer is swift of motion, so, too, the Land of Israel is swift to ripen its fruit.**

The Maharal speaks of the **vitality** of the land; he relates to the land like a living entity. When the people of Israel are living in the land, the land itself returns to life. Of all nations, the Master of

---

5   **Netzah Yisrael**, Chap. 6.

the Universe gave this land only to us because there is an inherent match between it and us, similar to the match between a husband and wife. Other nations have tried to gain a foothold here, but they have all failed[6]; the land waited for us like a woman waiting for her beloved husband; she refuses her favors to anyone else. It is precisely the unusual speed of the material development of the Land of Israel that is an indication that the Land of Israel possesses a quality that is **not** material, that it is the sanctity of the land that is at work here.

C. A good, broad, and expanding land

In tractate *Gittin* the simile of the deer is explained in a different way[7]. At the end of a description of a certain district in Judea, where a fantastically large number of residents are depicted as living, the gemara continues with an account of a skeptic who said to Rabbi Hanina that it was impossible that there were so many enormously populated cities in such a small geographical area. Rabbi Hanina's response was:

> *It is called 'Eretz Hatzvi'. Just as the skin of a deer [after it was removed from the deer's body] cannot contain the flesh of the deer [because it is stretched so tightly over the deer's body during its lifetime], so too, when the Jewish people are living in the Land, it expands, and when they are not living in it – it shrinks.*

6   "What was stated here ‹and your enemies who dwell in it shall be laid waste› is a glad tiding that declares that during all of our dispersions, our land does not receive our enemies. It is also a great proof and promise to us; this because you will not find anywhere in the civilized world a land which is good and bountiful which had been settled at one time and then became and remained barren as was the Land of Israel. The fact is that ever since its own People left it, it did not accept any nation or people; they all try to settle it and they are incapable". **Ramban on the Torah**, Lev. 26:15.
7   **Talmud Bavli**, *Gittin* 57a.

They say that people whose job it is to skin deer find it hard to fathom how this skin could have contained an entire deer. The skin looks too small, and yet when it is "worn" by the deer, it seems to grow as if it were made of an elastic material. So, too, the Land of Israel, which seems like a rather small country. Every time I point out the size of the Land of Israel on the globe to my children, they find it hard to accept its tiny dimensions. The gemara says that even so, when the people of Israel are living in the Land of Israel, it expands. It has room and the more Jews who come to live here – the **more room** there will be, not because of the success of wartime tactics but because that is the special nature of the Land of Israel: that it can expand, as it were, according to need.

The Maharal explains these words of the gemara following the passage (explaining the gemara in *Ketubot*) previously quoted:

> **The Holy Land, when its [rightful] residents are living in it, only then it has a transcendent excellence, which is that it is not limited in space; because it is physical matter that has a limit and a finite measure, but something that is transcendent is not finite like that which is material. Everything that is linked to transcendent, Divine sanctity is less limited than that which is wholly material, and that is why the Land of Israel, seen from the perspective of its having a transcendent aspect, is not limited in space because it does not have the restrictiveness and limitation that defines that which is material.**

Everything that is material has a limit and measure, a defined extent and a maximum velocity. Therefore any development that is fundamentally material – has necessarily a limited pace. But the Land of Israel has a 'transcendent excellence', it has tremendous spiritual energies that push forward its growth and development, and therefore the results are much beyond the limitations characteristic of mere material processes. This land, that has borders like any country, is spacious and has no limitations.

This property appears more forcefully in the place which is the qualitative essence of the Land of Israel: the Temple Mount with the *Beit Hamikdash*. In tractate *Yoma* it is written that one of the miracles that was done for the Jewish people when they went up to Jerusalem for the festivals, was that [as they stood in the courtyard of the *Beit Hamikdash*,] "they would stand pressed together, but when they bowed, there was room for all"[8] – in other words, there was great crowding while they were standing and logically, when they bowed, it should have been only more crowded, since bowing takes up more surface space, but on the contrary, when they bowed – there was suddenly room for all. This may be explained in an abstract way, thus: the decision to relate to the Land of Israel as a spiritual place, which is expressed in bowing down, creates an expansion. The land relates to us as we relate to it. If we treat it like a material place only, then the pace at which it operates is material; the more we relate to the Land of Israel as a holy place, as our spiritual life-partner, the faster is its pace of development.

In the *Birkat Hamazon* (grace after meals) too, we thank Hashem for the "desirable, good, and spacious land" – although it is hard to see the Land of Israel as a land that is spacious in terms of its physical dimensions. We understand that expanse is not only a physical matter but rather a matter of perspective, of approach. When we approach the Land of Israel as the land that is holy, it truly becomes spacious!

We will summarize this source using Roi's summary of the words of the Maharal:

> *The land of the deer as the ideal situation of the Jewish people: a spacious land – it has something expansive and G-dly in it because what transcends*

---

8   **Talmud Bavli**, *Yoma* 21a.

matter is not restricted, like the skin of the deer which is not similar in size to the deer itself: It is small and you can't understand how it once fit [the deer].

D. The land of peace

These sources from the gemara and the Maharal's explanation of them introduce us to a different relationship than is customary to the material and quantitative aspects of the Land of Israel. One should regard the development of the country and its affluence not as a normal, natural physical process but rather as an expression of spiritual strengths, of a very great spiritual vitality and a special blessing from Hashem.

The increase of Jews in the Land of Israel, its economic prosperity, the building of settlements, and laying of infrastructure – all of this proliferation holds spiritual significance, and as Roi phrased it:

*Proliferation and abundance in Israel reveal a Divine quality; it emerges that this abundance is not just more matter, but when it comes to Israel, it can only be **more spirit**. This [like the physical actions mandated by the mitzvot] is the body of the Torah, the appearance of Hashem's word, structured to fit the world, that Jewish building and endeavor carried out with a G-d-directed objective - this is spirit, it is not physical action. Therefore, these actions are not governed by the laws of physics [see Orot, last page].*

In his summary Roi refers to the words of Rav Kook at the end of the book *Orot*[9]:

> **In the Land of Israel, one can understand how the physicality of the Israeli body is holy, just like the holiness of the soul, and it is not so necessary to goad the body out of its natural repose, but instead to elevate it and to let it taste of the truth of a life of holiness that emanates from the holiness of the land, imbued with the 'air of the Land of Israel that makes one wise'.**

This is the uniqueness of the Land of Israel, of which Rabbi Yehuda Halevi wrote: "The lives of the souls are the air of your land" – it is only in the Land of Israel that material development is also spiritual development, and consequently it is possible in the Land of Israel to "make peace" between spirit and matter, because in the Land of Israel, spirit and matter are not antagonists to each other. The material existence of the Land of Israel draws its abundance from the holiness of the land, and over this, we recite the blessing, [the *Bracha Aharona* after certain food]: "Bring us up into it and gladden us in its rebuilding and let us eat from its fruit and be satisfied with its goodness". Generally, we associate a drive for satiation with excessive appetite and gluttony, but in finding satisfaction in the fruits of the land, there is also a spiritual dimension which is what we intend when we recite the blessing.[10]

Here we encounter a 'generous eye', a very profoundly positive perspective, the stretching out of a friendly hand from the source of holiness to the entire field of material and economic growth in the

---

9   **Orot**, Orot Yisrael, XI, 8 (p. 171).

10   "This land is holy, and when the 'Hatam Sofer' (Rabbi Moshe Sofer) determined in words of holiness that the fruits of the Land of Israel are "the holy fruits" of the land, it is not a figure of speech but rather it is deep wisdom which the 'Hatam Sofer' fully understood. The land is holy and its fruits are holy. There is sanctity in this banana and in this tomato, in this leaf, in this branch. And there is sanctity in this footpath, that seems when viewed superficially to be like any other in any place outside of Israel". **Sihot Harav Zvi Yehuda** on the Land of Israel p. 266.

Land of Israel. We recite a blessing over the material flourishing that takes place in the Land of Israel because it is growth that contains within it holiness, and it comes with such abundance because by nature the People of Israel are suited to the Land of Israel. When we are here, the life of holiness in the land flows rapidly, like the flight of the deer. It is noteworthy that despite the fact that the deer runs at a very high speed – sometimes even as high as eighty kilometers (50 miles) an hour – its flight is very delicate. It does not arouse fear or revulsion, it is not unpleasant or aggressive, but rather has something very beautiful and delicate about it. Likewise, the deer does not trample anything in the course of its flight. That is why the deer serves as an inspiration for the model of very rapid development which at the same time is not dizzying, that does not cause the kind of intoxication which ultimately leads to a fall. It is possible to develop rapidly and yet at the same time in a refined way; it is all a matter of the approach that one takes.

E. A pure economy

In the next passage, basing himself on the continuation of the words of the Maharal, Roi adds a key word in understanding our proper connection with the material development in the Land of Israel:

> There was a holiness of natural life in the Land of Israel. Economic life was run according to Jewish ideas of modesty. That was the nature of life – safeguarding the purity of growth, and when there is no purity, there is no economy.

The word 'purity' is the key word in understanding our very ability to experience material and economic growth as a spiritual phenomenon. The concept 'purity' appears many times in relation to the Land of Israel. The Torah warns us in several places against defiling the land because whoever defiles the land brings upon himself the punishment of being exiled from it[11]. The Land of Israel is also called a pure place, in contrast to the lands of the other nations which the sages decreed impure[12].

What is purity? How is it different from the concept of 'holiness'? Both of these words sound like they have a similar meaning, but we see that in the six sections of the Mishnah, they represent two different sections, one is called *'Seder Kodashim*, which comes from the word kedusha (=holiness) and the other is called *Seder Taharot*, whose root word is *tahara* (=purity). In what way are these two sets of laws different from each other? **Seder Kodashim** deals mainly with a person who wants to make a pilgrimage to the *Beit Hamikdash* for the purpose of prayer and sacrifice, which is parallel in our present-day reality to a person who dedicates some of his time to go to the synagogue or to the *beit midrash*. This means leaving everyday, mundane life in order to elevate oneself to spirituality. *Kedusha* is, then, setting oneself apart from the mundane, everyday routine for the sake of something higher, like Shabbat, which is called 'Shabbat Kodesh'. However, the challenge for anyone who has been privileged to advance to the level of *kodesh* is the return to the routine of daily life. Any person who has merited any measure of *kedusha* is concerned with the question of how will he be able to integrate this holiness into the wider circles of his life. Here is where the concept of purity enters. **Seder Taharot** does not deal with the question of people who come to the *Beit Hamikdash* but rather of those who live their ordinary life in the aspiration to have it connected to holiness with a connection that allows a constant absorption of that influence.

An example of this: we are familiar with various expressions that are based on the word *'tahara'* such as: *taharat hadibur* - purity of speech; *taharat ha-ma'asim* - purity of action; and

---

11 See e.g. **Lev.** 18: 24-30.
12 **Talmud Bavli**, *Shabbat* 14b.

taharat hamachshava - purity of thought. When a person is in the synagogue, it is taken for granted that he will be speaking about matters connected to holiness, but what happens when he leaves? Outside the synagogue one cannot always speak only of holy things. **Purity of speech** is the ability to scrupulously ensure that talk about ordinary matters is appropriate, harmonious with those moments when we spoke about holy things. Purity is the concord between all planes of life and the content of holiness, this, as opposed to impurity, which is the antithesis of holiness. Even if it is impossible to always speak exclusively about holy matters, it is possible to make an effort that speech about non-holy things should not be in contradiction to that which is holy. Purity is the attempt to achieve harmony between our ordinary life and our life of holiness.

Another example is **purity of thought**. It is clear that a person thinks of Torah while he is engaged in Torah study, but when he closes the books, his brain goes on working and his mind is taken up with things in the world other than Torah... Purity is the link and the harmonization between man's everyday thoughts and his thoughts when he is studying Torah. It is not right that a person's holy thoughts and his worldly thoughts be like two separate, unconnected worlds. One must strive for purity so that our ordinary thoughts are also connected in some measure to holiness. Purity goes hand in hand with unity, with the will to unite all of the different spheres of life with holiness, which is at the center of life. When an entire nation tries to live in purity, it is privileged to develop the land, its economic life flourishes because it succeeds in integrating holiness into all systems of life, and consequently, Hashem's blessing rests on that nation's endeavors.

Eretz Yisrael presents us with a challenge to build a prospering economy, and at the same time, **a pure one**. The language of this land, even when we are discussing economics, is the language of purity. Naturally we advocate relevant economic thinking but at the same time, we believe that it is possible to build a pure economy, and thus to merit a tremendous blessing, affluence that is unequaled. In a pure economy, there is room for thinking that is not based only on what I am **taking** from the other person but also what I am **giving** him. In a pure economy, wealth and growth are not allocated to the person who trampled his fellowman but rather to the one who ran forward like a deer – swiftly but without riding roughshod over anyone. In such an economic system, thinking about the general welfare is a key component, as opposed to an economy whose entire purpose is to satisfy the appetites of individuals.

F. A pure army

One of the organizations where maintaining purity is particularly difficult is the army. In the army, the sense of the material power and the extent of preoccupation with material matters are extreme. That is because materialism and physicality surround the soldiers twenty-four hours a day, and all of the parameters by which success and failure are measured are physical ones: who runs faster, who is stronger, which unit carries out an assignment more successfully, more quickly, and more forcefully. Therefore the army jargon contains many expressions that are taken from the animal world, because the army is a place where physical power reaches its starkest dimensions, and there can be something animal-like in that. Furthermore, the army possesses extreme instruments of material force; the simple soldier may find himself wielding tremendous power in his hands, whether an armored vehicle like an APC or a tank, or a weapons systems that can wreak a huge amount of devastation and destruction with the highest intensity and precision. Thus it is easy to become rough and aggressive while in the army, qualities antithetical to spirituality and refinement. However, anyone who is able to adopt for himself the attribute of purity – receives strength from the holiness of the Land of Israel and not only is he able to meet the professional standards demanded of him but he is more successful than others, and he discovers abilities and strengths in an immense range of fields. The

Land favors him until even his earthly, physical abilities grow and he flourishes and succeeds, even in the purely military sense. Purity of this kind was the secret of Roi's success in the army.

Although, in the exile, the concept of purity was the province of only a select few, in our generation it is set to expand, as Rav Kook said of the "healthy nucleus" at the core of the aspiration [of *Hassidut*] to plant the ideal of purity in the general population[13]:

> **It is particularly right that it become greater together with the renaissance of the nation in the Land of Israel…"When you go out to encamp against your enemies, keep yourself from every evil thing. If there be among you any man who is not clean by reason of uncleanness that chances by night, then he shall go out of the camp; he shall not come within the camp (Deut. 23)."**

The Torah commanded us to intensify our insistence on purity precisely when we are in a military setting. In the synagogue, a man who is not clean is allowed to be present, but not in a military camp, because it is there, of all places – in the encounter with the physical might that the army represents – that we are obliged to increase purity.

> **Wherever broad-based Israeli strength intensifies, it is imperative that an intensification of physical and emotional purity immediately follow, with all of its qualities, to bond with it, and all of these [strength, purity and its associated qualities] prepare a basis for a living, organic order which embraces the full stature of the national renaissance, beginning at the top with the heights of abstract thought and ending at the bottom with the simplest of life's gaieties and**

---

13 **Orot**, *Orot Ha-tehiya*, 35 [p. 81].

the thunder of life's strength. "And I will set glory [in Hebrew: "tzvi" which as we have seen means also "deer"] in the land of the living [=the Land of Israel]" (Ezekiel 26).

G. The inner truth of the Land

To live that part of life which is ordinary and mundane in purity by constantly drawing upon the values of the holy, does not turn us into people who are not living in the "real world"; on the contrary: that is how we live in the "real world" with greater intensity. Purity is a vessel that enables us to thoroughly utilize to the fullest the treasure of life that lies stored in holiness.

The love of the Jewish people for the Land of Israel is different than the love of other nations for their land. Certainly every nation develops a natural connection to its homeland, and certainly every person loves the landscapes of the land where he grew up and which he knows. But our connection to the Land of Israel is completely different; this land is a fountain of life for us, a place where we encounter the holiness that exists within us. This land enables us to reconcile our spiritual desires with our material desires. Through the land it is possible "to understand how the physicality of the Israeli body is holy just as much as the holiness of the soul". Therefore there is no contradiction for us between a personality that is refined and spiritual who regularly devotes time to the study of Torah and a personality characterized by martial power, who has an understanding of the economy. It is not a contradiction, because in the depth of our lives it is truly the same thing, by virtue of two inner truths that so characterized Roi: the love of the Land and purity. When these two inner truths exist in the soul and work their influence upon it, there is no room for the question of how is it that there is a person who both studies Torah at the highest level and is also an outstanding combat officer; it all represents one composition because the material development of the Land of Israel is the body of Torah, as Roi wrote in the passage quoted earlier.

H. The consolations of the Land of Israel

When one's relationship to the Land of Israel is only functional, a surprising thing happens: although it is quite a small country, it suddenly seems to many people to be too big, and they begin to think that we do not need so much of our own land, that we can "go on a diet" to reduce the Land of Israel and to "liberate ourselves" of the parts that we do not need so much. On the other hand, when we elevate ourselves to the point where we relate to the Land of Israel as the Holy Land, it becomes beloved for itself and every meter of it becomes more precious than jewels, just as each letter of the Torah scroll is precious and essential. From every small bit of the Land of Israel we draw the strength of holiness.

We will soon enter the period of 'Yemei ben ha-metzarim'* when we are preoccupied with the memory of the exile. The exile was the consequence of our looking at the land without remembering that it is the Holy Land; therefore, the greatest correction we can make to eliminate the cause for the era of exile is to repeat to ourselves endlessly that we do not live in a normal country, but in the Holy Land. How happy that makes us and how wondrous that is. With that understanding we should be filled with joy over every development of the country, every planting and every house that is built. Adopting an approach that causes us to be filled with a fierce love for every good thing that develops in the land – like the sense

---

* The three weeks between the fast of the 17th of Tamuz and Tisha B'av, the period of mourning over the destruction of both Temples and the exile of the Jewish people from its land.

of happiness that floods those who love Torah whenever they learn something new – this rectifies a wrong by erasing the reason for the destruction.

In the last paragraph of Orot, Rav Kook writes[14]:

> **It is a mitzvah to taste fully of the pleasurable sweetness of the radiance of the vibrant holiness of the Land of Israel. So that you may eat to satisfaction and suckle upon the breast of its consolations, that you may extract and enjoy the radiance of its glory[15].**

The land has its consolations with which it consoles us over the long exile, and in order to earn those consolations, we must learn to know the Land of Israel in its holiness, its purity, and its wholeness.

There are people – and Roi was an outstanding example of such – for whom everything discussed here is not mere words but is real life, and it is from these people that we must take an example. With Hashem's help, all parts of the Land of Israel – to which we are tied with a strong soul-connection – will one day revert to our full sovereignty. It is no coincidence that we are endlessly preoccupied with struggles over different parts of the Land of Israel. Even when the Jewish people want to escape various parts of the land, the Master of the Universe ensures that we will be unable to disengage ourselves completely, and we find ourselves returning to them all the time, if not by choice then under duress. This, of course, does not exempt our enemies from their rightful punishment for their viciousness and their aggressiveness, but along with this reckoning, we must regard these struggles as a reminder from the Master of the Universe that we have parts of life that are not yet in our hands.

---

14 **Orot**, Orot Yisrael 9,9 [p. 171].
15 A paraphrase of **Isa**. 66:11.

Sizable parts of southern Lebanon also belong to us; they are the tribal inheritance of Dan and Asher. Beyond the fact that this is part of the Divine promise, there actually had been Jewish settlement in southern Lebanon. When we met the man who served as Head of the Northern Command during the Second War in Lebanon, General Udi Adam, who came to Eli, he spoke in this spirit. I asked him if he had any special feelings during the war, since twenty-four years earlier, his father General Yekutiel Adam, former Deputy Chief of Staff of the Israeli Defense Forces, had been killed during the Peace for Galilee Operation (the First Lebanon War) on Lebanese soil. After he replied that his feelings were indeed very charged, he added that apparently we have something there in southern Lebanon and he began to describe for us the Biblical sources for a Jewish presence in that area. The General finished up by saying that that must be the reason that we keep finding ourselves back there again and again.

When we learn to see all parts of our land – including those that are not in our hands at the present – as bits of holiness, bits of life, when we know how to approach them in purity, they will illuminate our path and give us strength and blessing. Because it is our perspective on the Land that determines the way that it relates back to us.

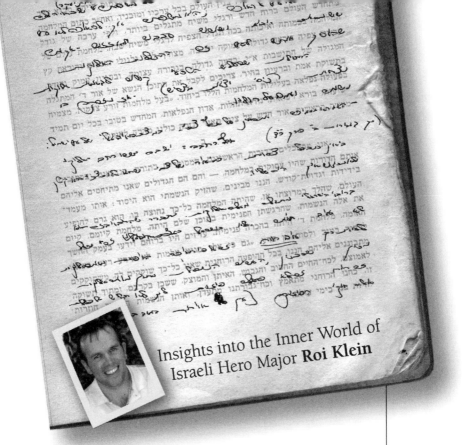

Insights into the Inner World of
Israeli Hero Major **Roi Klein**

Chapter 9

Charity as a national endeavor

Charity as a national endeavor

A. Organized charity

B. David's kingdom of Hesed

C. Private *tzedaka* as a temporary substitute

D. "Zion shall be redeemed through *tzedaka*"

E. *Tzedaka* with dignity

F. Giving the poor a share in the mitzvah of *'Pe'ah'**

G. The necessity of poverty in the world

H. It is the giver who profits

A. *Organized hesed*

When Roi was sent by the army to study for his BA, he chose to study Industrial Engineering and Management. Although during those years his Torah study took priority over his university studies, he was successful in both areas, and he graduated with honors. As a condition for receiving his degree, he was required to submit a final paper. It is accepted practice in this field to write a paper proposing a business plan to maximize the efficiency of a business corporation. Roi and his thesis partner, Benny Kuperman, thought that instead of writing a standard paper, it would be more beneficial to write a proposal for improving the operations of a charitable organization. They attached themselves to the charitable organization 'Koach Latet' [The power to give] which collects second-hand equipment – household furnishings and appliances – and distributes it to the needy. There they learned about the operating procedures of the organization, and wrote a precedent-setting paper in which they applied classical models of industrial engineering and management to a charitable organization.

---

* leaving a corner of the field for the poor.

Beyond the powerful statement made by this choice of a topic, it is enlightening to read the introduction to the paper written by Roi, an introduction that encapsulates an entire worldview:

The field of Industrial Engineering and Management deals primarily with the analysis and streamlining of different systems: employees, machines, and the relationship between them; sales, inventory, marketing, organizational hierarchies, and the like. But while we usually analyze and try to streamline systems that belong to economic or government corporations, it is also possible to try to maximize the efficiency of organizations that deal with charity and *hesed*, and to create a system of organized *hesed*. After all, the principal uniqueness and essence of the Jewish people is the world of *hesed*, justice, honesty, and goodness – "From the very inception of this people...there was manifested the aspiration to establish a great human collective that would 'keep the way of G-d to do righteousness and justice'." (Rav Kook, Orot, *Le'mahalach ha-ideo't b'Yisrael* II). So how is it that when we come to deal with a profession that was designed specifically to improve, to upgrade, and to excel, that we neglect the world of *hesed*, of all things?!

A state of affairs where the industrial world in all of its various branches is accorded managerial attention, in streamlining systems at the highest rates of resolution, while on the other hand, the world of *hesed* remains neglected in terms of professional management tactics, where it is amateur, unprofessional and disorganized – that is a patently unreasonable situation. The commandments to give charity and to perform deeds of *hesed* must be treated no less seriously and professionally, and even more so – than any other of life's professions. The finest Israeli minds in the field of industry and management must invest their best talents and energies precisely here, in the world that is so characteristic of Israel, the world of *hesed* and charity.

This project is an attempt to create a gateway and a bridge to connect the world of *hesed* with basic models from the world of industry and management. We hope that many other students, lecturers, and professionals will follow in this path and help charitable organizations become a "pillar of fire" in the professional arena, because of the values of *hesed* that define them.

An idea which can be developed from Roi's introduction, one which we want to discuss in this meeting, is that we should not be satisfied to have charitable work carried out only by individuals but we must aspire to constructing general systems which will be mobilized for the lofty purpose of doing *tzedaka* and *hesed*. Charity must be part of a decision-making process. From here one might continue one step further: it must be one of the considerations on the national agenda, *tzedaka* that is civic and state-based – and it must be part of the way of thinking of the state, as a state.

B. David's kingdom of Hesed

The perception that *tzedaka* is a commandment that must be performed at the level of the national collective has ideological sources; one of these is the way our sages portray the kingdom of David, of whom it was said:

And David reigned over all of Israel, and David

> *executed judgment (mishpat) and charity (tzedaka) to*
> *all his people.[1]*

David was involved in *tzedaka* in his role as king; not the kind of
tzedaka that is part of a ruler's public relations but as policy, as part
of his royal leadership.

The midrash takes this one step further in interpreting the
verse:

> *If he saw a poor man whom his beit din (court that*
> *rules in accordance to halacha) determined was*
> *obligated to pay money, [David] would repay it out*
> *of his own funds. He executed 'judgment' (mishpat) –*
> *to the claimant who received the money that he was*
> *owed, and charity (tzedaka) – to the poor man whom*
> *David repaid out of his own personal funds.[2]*

David's military commander, who today would be called the
Minister of Defense, was Yoav ben Zeruyah, of whom it was said
that he was buried "in his house in the desert"[3]. Our sages ask about
this "Was his house truly in the desert?"

> *Rabbi Yehuda says in the name of Rav: "In the desert"*

---

1   **II Sam.** 8:15.

2   **Yalkut Shimoni**, II Sam. 147 [s.v. *Va-yehi David oseh*].
In **Talmud Bavli**, *Bava Batra* 10b: "They asked Shlomo son of David: How great is
the power of *tzedaka*? And he replied: Go and see how my father David interpreted
it: 'He has distributed freely, he has given to the poor, his righteousness endures for
ever; his power shall be exalted with honor' (Ps. 112:9)".
See also the **Ramban** on Lev. 20:17 who discusses *tzedaka* of the national collective
with reference to the words of Shlomo himself in the Book of Proverbs –"*Tzedaka*
exalts a nation but sin is a reproach to nationalities") Prov" :(14:34 .But in my
understanding ,the simple meaning of the verse is that '*tzedaka* exalts a nation' when
that nation performs it, and 'sin is a reproach to nationalities' – when they do not
perform *tzedaka*, because with tzedaka and *hesed* lie both the praise of every nation
and their downfall. Another explanation is that *Tzedaka* will exalt that special nation
that performs it but many nations sin when it comes to *hesed* and do not perform
it".

3   I **Kings** 2:34.

> *signifies that just as the desert belongs to no one and is*
> *thus open to all, so too was Yoav's house open to all.*"[4]

And so, it would seem that this was the atmosphere in the kingdom of the House of David: the civic leaders were involved in doing acts of charity, even to the point of opening their homes to all those in need.

C. Individual tzedaka as a temporary substitute

We know that the service of Hashem through sacrifices has a very prominent place in the Torah, but what shall we do in our generation when we have no *beit mikdash* and we cannot bring sacrifices? The gemara in tractate *Brachot* answers this question:

> *As long as the Beit Hamikdash was standing – the altar*
> *[sacrifices] atoned for the people of Israel; now in our*
> *day – it is Man's table that atones for him.*[5]

From the context of the gemara, it can be understood that the table of man can atone for him when he has the poor eating at his table by inviting them and supplying them with food. However, Rav Kook, in his commentary on the *agadot* of the gemara, tries to find a deeper connection between the table and the altar, between giving *tzedaka* and offering sacrifices[6]:

> And when the *Beit Hamikdash* was standing, when
> we were in a position of national strength both
> materially and spiritually, we could also found our
> charitable works on the collective, with worthy
> exalted institutions as suited to the importance of a

---

4 **Yalkut Shimoni** on I Kings, 172 [s.v. *'Va-yeshev Benayahu'*].
5 **Talmud Bavli**, *Brachot* 55a.
6 **Ein Aya**, Brachot, IX, 24.

> great nation encompassing the people's thoughts and
> desires. And the altar would atone for Israel – the
> altar: signifying the entire range of service of Hashem
> performed by Israel – which includes the improvement
> of our moral condition whether with regard to the
> relationship between man and G-d or between man
> and man. By virtue of the national collective, we could
> establish our institute of charity as a great endeavor.

For the Rav, the gemara is not necessarily referring to the actual
physical *Beit Hamikdash*, but to the period when Israel enjoyed
a full national life. The *Beit Hamikdash* where the nation makes
a pilgrimage, serves in this gemara as a symbol of a national
condition which is complete and operating properly, as a contrast
to a situation where each individual goes to pray in his own private
synagogue in his limited community. Indeed, our mourning over
the destruction of the *Beit Hamikdash* includes mourning over the
life of the sovereign state which we had and have lost. This national
integrity – whose revival we believe that we are now in the midst
of – enabled us to be involved in doing acts of *hesed* and charity at
the level of the nation. It takes a nation to carry out projects on a
colossal scale, on a national scope. Just as the altar belonged to the
nation as a whole, so too, is it appropriate that the commandment
relating to charity be carried out in an organized, nation-wide
mode.

> Now that the *Beit Hamikdash* is no longer in existence,
> and, because of our sins, the energies of the nation
> have been dispersed in all directions, …we must cling
> with all of our strength to the stronghold of simple,
> individual charity. A man's table atones for him when
> he distributes his bread to the poor in a simple and
> direct way, and the relationship between table and
> altar will teach us to understand this, inasmuch as the
> table is only a substitute for the altar. But when there

**is an altar, then we must yearn for the bond that brings
everyone together. Therefore it is right to remark
that if somehow at any time, we have a renewed
opportunity to administer our charitable endeavors
in a way that encompasses more than the individual,
and especially through a national association, then
the commandment upon us to do so is very great. This
because the individual can never achieve the great
things that the collective can effect. Therefore, the
greatest of the attributes of charity is to give to the
communal fund: the charity fund.**

The private table at which we feed the poor is only a temporary
replacement to enable us to be engaged in charity during periods
of exile as well, but our true aspiration is always to do charity
in its full sense, its national sense, charity that is organized and
institutionalized. When the conditions are created that will allow
this, we must make the effort to restore to the commandment of
charity its original, full status. The ability of individuals – even
those blessed with wealth and a generous inclination – cannot be
compared to the ability of a sovereign state, where the strength of
the entire public comes to expression.

**And even more so, when there is a forming of a
national tie that can reform many matters and save
many from poverty and need before it befalls them,
when communal charity becomes more like an altar
than like a table, then it is a *mitzvah* to help and be a
partner in this.**

The state has the power to prevent its citizens' decline into a state of
poverty and need, by building systems of civil support. It is a great
mitzvah to participate in the building of such systems, and a condition
for it is to marshal the country's finest minds with the aim of training
ourselves to this way of thinking, as expressed in Roi's introduction to
his paper.

D. "Zion shall be redeemed through tzedaka"

In light of these understandings, it is easier to understand why the gemara links the building of Jerusalem to the *mitzvah* of charity:

> **Ula said: Jerusalem will be redeemed only through charity, as written: "Zion shall be redeemed through justice (mishpat), and those that return to her through charity (tzedaka)"[7].**

Jerusalem is our capital city, and it is proper that a deep sense of national identity manifest itself there. To do that, the people of Israel must first define their national identity. When a nation does not have its own distinctive identity, it gradually fades away. All over the world people go to work every morning and return home at night. What then differentiates our nation from all of the others? Our uniqueness is that justice and charity are at the top of our national order of priorities, in that we want to build a prosperous economy where *hesed* and *tzedaka* are built-in integrally, because that is our fame and our glory.

It is important to understand that one can do charity in ways other than giving money; a person can give his fellowman of his time, his talents, or even his attention. Not everyone has enough money to give a lot of charity but everyone is capable of giving his fellowman generously of what he was blessed with. In recent years there has been a significant and welcome trend where people donate hours of work in the profession that they have been trained. For example, lawyers, in an organized way and on a voluntary basis, give legal advice to those who cannot afford it, or doctors receive a certain number of patients in their private clinics each week without a fee. The expansion of activity of this kind is a desirable phenomenon, especially when it is done in an organized manner,

---

7   **Talmud Bavli**, *Shabbat* 139a.

so that it also maintains the dignity of those who come to ask for help.

The performance of acts of charity is an expression of brotherhood and unity in the nation. The Maharal explains[8] that the stirring to help one's fellowman reveals the deep connections between individuals. In contrast, when a person turns a blind eye to an appeal for charity and lives his life in a private, egoistical way, he intensifies the alienation and the division within the nation. "Who is like Your people Israel, one nation in the land" – it is we of all nations who must be a nation where unity is our foremost ideal. Unity is the essence of our nation, and is closely connected to our belief in one G-d[9]. Therefore, the Maharal says in a homiletic style, the Hebrew word] "צדקה/tzedaka] is composed of letters that are adjacent to each other in the alphabet, letters that are like brothers: the *tzadi* with the *kuf* (that follows it in the alphabet), and the *dalet* with the *heh*. *Tzedaka* creates a closeness and connection between people who are distant from each other.

E. Tzedaka with dignity

We have seen, then, that from a practical aspect, *tzedaka* that is carried out in a way that is based on the national collective is better organized and more efficient; furthermore, spiritually, *tzedaka* expresses fidelity to our national identity and to the unity of the nation. However, another advantage of *tzedaka* when carried

8 **Netivot Olam**, Netiv Hatzedaka, chap. 2.
9 "Just as the idol worshiper denies the unity of the Holy One blessed be He, and believes that He shares power with another entity – so, too, the sin of controversy and schism among the people of Israel is the essence of denying the unity of the Holy One blessed be He, because the source of the unity of the Holy One blessed be He requires that the entire body of the people of Israel be united together in love, fellowship, and goodwill, bound together, adhering to each other without any division and rift...Even more than the unity of the body which is comprised of many limbs, because the unity of the people of Israel is testimony to the unity of the Holy One blessed be He." / **Beit David**, Rabbi David Tevil of Minsk, Drush 6.

out by the national collective: such *tzedaka* has a more **dignified** character. When a person gives charity individually, it usually causes a sense of embarrassment and sometimes even humiliation in the person who needs the charity. But *tzedaka* that is distributed by the state is perceived as something to which the poor person is entitled.

Our sources that discuss *tzedaka* attribute great importance to the matter of dignity in giving *tzedaka*. In tractate *Ketubot*[10], we learn that *tzedaka* performed the way it should be includes restoring the lost dignity of the needy person, and therefore one cannot be content to merely fill the physical needs of the poor person according to objective criteria but additionally, one must aspire to provide his need as he experiences it, taking into account his status before he declined into poverty:

> *"Whatever he lacks" – even a horse to ride and a servant to run before him. It was said of Hillel the Elder that he gave a poor man who had once been rich a horse to ride and a servant to run before him. Once he could not find a servant to run before him so he himself ran before the horse for three miles.*

We see that Hillel, who held high public office, was always concerned about the psychological needs of the needy person who apparently had once been well-off and respected. He took pains to make this poor man feel important.

When charity is based on the national collective, it possesses the means of preserving the dignity of those who need it.

---

10 **Talmud Bavli**, *Ketubot* 67b.

F. Giving the poor a share in the mitzvah of 'Pe'ah'

In the context of discussing the *mitzvah* of *tzedaka* that should be performed in a dignified way, the *mitzvah* of *pe'ah* is especially interesting: This *mitzvah* is mentioned in the Torah several times and is a central part of the Rambam's laws of giving charity. One of the places where it is mentioned in the Torah is the chapter of the festivals in the book of Leviticus; incidental to the commandment of the holiday of *Shavuot*, the harvest festival, the Torah repeats the obligation to leave the corner of the field for the poor[11]. On the surface, the commandment of *pe'ah* is altogether rather strange: The rich man has a field, orchard, or vineyard, he harvests his crop and leaves a certain portion as it is, without harvesting or reaping. He invites the poor people, each one brings his own scythe or pruning shears, and they come to the rich man's field in order to work. It would seem that instead of asking the poor people to work for themselves, it would be fitting for the field-owners to harvest for the poor and to hand out prepared baskets of fruit. Why does the Torah require the poor people to harvest for themselves?

In order to understand the reason, one must appreciate the atmosphere during the harvest season: this is the season when the difference between those who own fields and those who do not comes to its starkest expression. The harvest season is the finest hour of the field-owner. The rich man arrives at his large field and begins to reap with a heart brimming with joyful pleasure, filled with satisfaction over harvesting the product of his intensive labor of many months. The poor, not only do they not enjoy the product of the harvesting process – the wheat, grapes, or olives – but they also feel excluded, left on the margins of the great harvest season activity. Even if they are given some of the crops, this will not be compensation for the aggrieved feeling that they have for being

---

11 **Lev.** 23:22.

left outside the experience of the harvest. Therefore, the Torah says: Include the poor! Let him have some of the experience, let him feel that part of the field is really his! That way you restore his dignity. In this way the Torah wants us to be concerned not only about the poor person's physical needs but also about his status and his feelings.

It is not without cause that the commandment of *pe'ah* is a central element of the chapter on the festivals, within the section on *Shavuot*. On this holiday we read Megillat Ruth where the commandment of *pe'ah* plays an important role. In the Megilla we encounter – as we accompany Ruth going to glean in the field of Boaz – a living demonstration of the fulfillment of the commandment of *pe'ah*.

Pe'ah is associated not only with the agricultural aspect of *Shavuot* but also with the aspect of receiving the Torah. When the Torah was given, we were poor in the sense of being without the Torah, and the Master of the universe was like the rich man, who could give us the Torah. Hashem did not give it to us outright, as one who spoon-feeds a baby, but He said to us: The Torah is yours, and like with the field, if the farmer wants to see results, he must work; so too the Torah demands that that we exert ourselves at in-depth study and interpretation, questions and answers. That is how Hashem made us partners in His Torah. In this context the Ramhal quotes the verse from Ecclesiastes (*Kohelet*): "A king makes himself a servant to the field (Ecc. 5:8) – the nation is a partner with its King in its spiritual field work, in studying the Torah of Israel.

G. The necessity of poverty in the world

The tractate of *Pe'ah* deals broadly not with just the obligation to give to the poor but also how it should be done, so that the poor person acquires not only money but also dignity. For example: one of the *mishnayot* states that a person who does not allow the poor to collect the *pe'ah* in his field is violating the injunction[12]: "Remove not the ancient landmark", which means that the poor person has tangible rights in your property, to the point where if you do not allow him entry, you are considered a trespasser on property that presumably was yours! Rav Kook makes a comment on this mishnah which is important to our understanding of the way we must approach doing charity at the national level[13]:

> **Anyone who thinks that the creation has an absolute flaw is already far from understanding the supreme ways of Hashem, "He is the Rock, His work is perfect"; there is no misfortune in the world that was prepared unless some beneficial purpose may emerge from it, and the depiction of something as unfortunate is possible only from the individual's limited view of the short-term, but over the universality of time and reality, everything joins together for good.**

When we are exposed to negative phenomena in the reality we live, along with the war we must wage against them and the sorrow that we must feel, it is right that one also elevate himself to a higher sphere and understand that from a perspective that is higher than Man's, from Hashem's perspective, even the evil ultimately serves a beneficial purpose. So, too, in the painful and distressing phenomenon of poverty, there is surely a spark of good, something positive that emerges as a result of it.

---

12 **Prov.** 23:10.
13 **Ein Aya**, Pe'ah, 2

> And so it is with the attribute of poverty, for surely
> many good qualities result from it: improving human
> qualities and softening the hardness of one's heart,
> and the very tendency to volunteer and participate in
> the sorrow of another person, and the actualization
> of the love of that which is good and kind, precious
> qualities, which – when they are joined to the crown
> of Mind and true knowledge – ennoble the human
> soul raising it in a very precious exaltation, and they
> come to be activated only by the reality of poverty.

The presence of poor people in the world requires that those with means must realize the potential of their qualities of compassion and *hesed*, and in this way to become more human. Because poverty exists, people express many positive forces that they possess within themselves.

> And many such good things are unknown to us, to the
> point where the poor people through their poverty
> also take part in the general enterprise of mankind, to
> bring the world to the attainment of its happy purpose
> like all the other agents.

According to this fresh way of thinking offered by Rav Kook, the poor are not just a burden on society; they also contribute to the advancement of society by their very existence, by obliging society to be better and more generous, less egoistical.

> Therefore the gift the Torah allocates to them must be
> given in the sense of what justice requires, as one gives
> something to someone who takes what is rightfully
> his, and not in the sense of undeserved beneficence
> and mercy.

The contribution of the poor is so great that the person who gives charity should not feel at all that he is "doing a favor" to the poor person, but rather that his act is appropriate and called for by justice, and that he is actually paying for a "service" that he receives from the poor person: the improvement of his character.

> **And the clearest example of the necessity of the existence of poverty to advance the general reform of the world is the fact that it has always existed and is widespread. "The ancient landmark", something that has existed over time in human nature, cannot be without an objective included in the purpose of Divine Providence.**

Despite many attempts, no economic system in the world has ever succeeded in totally eradicating the phenomenon of poverty, as it is written in the Torah: "For the poor shall not cease out of the land"[14]. The fact that this phenomenon persists should teach us about the necessity of the existence of poverty in our world. Poverty is a law of G-d, and although there are no volunteers for this assignment, Divine Providence arranges reality so that every society will always have a certain percentage of people who need the help of others in order to survive. There is a far-reaching truth in this: that if there were no poor people in the world, it would be necessary to invent them because society needs the needy.

> **Therefore, anyone whose actions express a contrary conception, who does not allow the poor to harvest *pe'ah* from his field, although he gives them of his fruit, is nonetheless destroying the foundation, which is that he must recognize that they are not be being given something they do not deserve, but they, like he, are entitled to what is justly theirs, to partake of what is their own... But what must become ingrained is the principle is that there is no flaw in the work of Hashem, and the quality of scarcity and poverty**

---

14 **Deut.** 15:11.

have a purpose in reality which only the poor can fulfill, and it is most marked in the improvement of character which leads to the improvement of one's deeds, so that we are saved by the [poor] from the punishment of Gehenna. That is why "you shall not remove an ancient landmark".

In light of this, it is appropriate that our thinking about the issue of doing *hesed* and charity should not be aimed at the total eradication of poverty (something which is impossible) but rather focused on the idea of how to give more; the emphasis should be placed on the very act of giving, not on looking for a pragmatic solution that will free us once and for all from the problem of world poverty[15].

Practicing charity should not be carried out with of a sense of condescension but instead, with a feeling of respect for the poor person, and this respect is born only in the moment that you realize that it is **he** who is giving to **you**. In meeting him, you have left the "bubble" that surrounded you, you have sharpened your awareness of the plight of your fellowman, you have thought about something other than yourself. Anyone engaged in the *mitzvah* of charity – even to a small extent – discovers generally that he is becoming more refined in his personal life, that something within him is softening. Such a person profits greatly, not economically but psychologically. Following this thinking, it is easy to understand the words of the Rambam on the mishna[16] where he writes that a

---

15 Editor's note: This lecture does not recommend the kind of giving that perpetuates poverty. It is right to try to extricate the poor person from the cycle of poverty. The point is that even after sincere efforts, poverty as such will not be totally eradicated, since it has a role to play in the world of the Holy One, blessed be He.

16 **Rambam**'s commentary on Pirkei Avot ch.3 mishna 15.
Editor's note: Of course, someone performing the mitzvah of *tzedaka* who thinks – not of fulfilling Hashem's commandment, nor about his obligation to assist the poor person – but rather, egotistically, of how it is he who is going to benefit by improving his own character traits, is not performing the mitzvah in the best way (see Hilchot Teshuva ch. 10). One improves his character traits by acting out of concern for his fellow-man; not by calculating how he himself will benefit. If one were confronted therefore with a choice between two options of *tzedaka* the determining factors

person who gives a thousand coins to a thousand different poor people, each needing just the one coin, refines his own character traits through his acts of giving more extensively than another who gives the same amount all at once to one poor person who needs all one thousand coins. The first donor participates in the experience of giving a thousand times over.

H. It is the giver who profits

When an entire country adopts this way of thinking, not only will the poor benefit, the entire country will benefit. It has a tremendous educational value. That is why it is important that part of the educational training in the schools, in youth movements, and even at the universities include giving to one's fellowman, and wherever this is possible, even arriving at the creation of new, more sophisticated mechanisms for performing the mitzvah of *tzedaka*.

A short time ago we met with Dudi Zilbershlag, the executive director of the charitable organization 'Koah Latet', who said to us explicitly that all of the principals of educational institutions whom he met, who took part regularly in projects involving *tzedaka*, reported concomitant educational gains, such as a drop in the level of their pupils' *hutzpa* and aggressive behavior, and a rise in sensitivity and consideration for their friends. These pupils lost a bit of their free time but gained sevenfold educationally and emotionally.

Roi charted a path for us in the paper that he wrote with Benny and with the totality of his life – which was a continuum of giving

---

would be objective – how many people were benefited and how acute was their duress. In this light it is worth noting that community or national-collective based charity, where each individual contributes to a general fund, reduces the number of acts of individual giving and yet Rav Kook favors this option.

in different spheres – and we must continue it by developing more sophisticated systems of charitable works, building efficient structures of counseling and support, and connecting the talents of different professionals who want to give with the diverse needs of those in need. In this way we can also integrate into the cycle of giving those who want to help but economically find it hard. It will begin with organizations and local initiatives, which are already steadily increasing and will eventually reach – so we anticipate and believe – the level of national thinking and the formulation of a national economic policy that places giving to the weak sectors of society at the top of our national priorities.

As we make advances in this direction, so too shall our national identity become increasingly clear. *Hesed*, the desire to benefit all, to benefit the entire world, is central to our identity as a nation[17] since the days of our forefather Avraham, whose entire essence was love for his fellowman, giving, and *hesed*. We cannot escape the tent of Avraham, which is open on all four sides: that is where we came from and that is where we will return[18], as a whole nation that is executing justice and charity in the land.

---

17 "The very will to be good to everyone, without any limit in the world at all, not in regard to the number of beneficiaries nor to the quality of the benefit bestowed, this is the inner nucleus of the essence of the soul of *Knesset Yisrael*. This is the heritage of its forefathers. This feeling of goodness, in proportion to its magnitude, breadth and depth, needs to be crowned with a great wisdom and a strong power of perseverance in order to know how to realize itself in all of its aspects. And this is what is hidden in the longing of the nation for its redemption, a longing which gives it the power to live and to survive in a way that astonishes the heart of any thinking person". / **Orot**, Orot Yisrael I, 4.

18 **Jer**. 23:5 "Behold, the days come, says G-d, that I will raise a righteous shoot for David, and he shall reign as king and prosper, and he shall execute justice (*mishpat*) and charity (*tzedaka*) in the land."

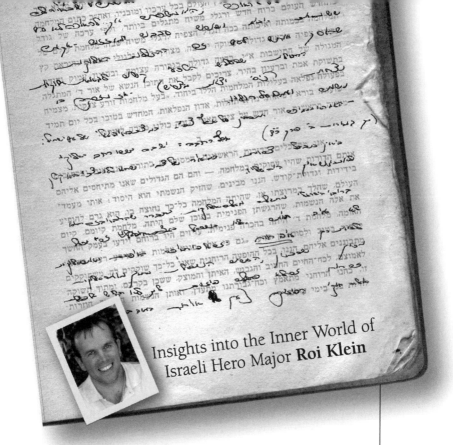

Insights into the Inner World of
Israeli Hero Major **Roi Klein**

Major Roi Klein, Hero of Israel

A short biography

Major Roi Klein, Hero of Israel

A short biography

Roi [pronounced: Ro-ee] Klein, the son of Aharon and Shoshana Klein, and the brother of Yifat and Noa, was born on the 2nd of Av 5735 (1975). Roi attended the 'Yavneh' elementary school in Ra'anana and then went on to study in the Ra'anana Bnei Akiva Yeshiva Junior High School. As a child, Roi was shy, sensitive, and extraordinarily talented. He was brought up to excel and to strive for greatness, and was endowed with a large measure of creative imagination and curiosity.

In his teenage years, Roi was very involved in the activity of the local chapter of the Bnei Akiva youth organization, first as a member and later as a counselor. The idealistic atmosphere that reigned within his local chapter of Bnei Akiva as a whole, and in particular within the age group to which Roi belonged, and his counselors – some of whom later became Torah scholars and outstanding officers in the IDF – left a significant imprint on Roi's character. At that time he was noted for the combination of a sharp, healthy sense of humor when among his friends and for his intense seriousness, atypical of someone his age, in everything relating to tasks that he had undertaken: reading [as part of the synagogue service] the entire Torah with the cantillations and playing the piano and the saxophone. His pealing laughter became his trademark. Roi was endowed with dramatic talent and in the various plays and performances put on at the Bnei Akiva chapter, he would shed his shyness, go up on stage, and make the audience laugh until they had tears in their eyes. Roi was always very careful not to hurt anyone with his humor and never turned it against others in an insulting way. During this period love for Eretz Yisrael blossomed within him and he would go on hikes all over the country, visiting its footpaths, its mountains, and its streams. Even during the stormy period of adolescence, and certainly afterwards, Roi was always scrupulous in observing the commandment to honor his father and mother.

Roi completed his high school studies at the technological yeshiva affiliated with Bar-Ilan University and excelled in his studies. He completed his matriculation exams in mathematics by the end of the tenth grade and while still a high school student, managed to take several courses in mathematics at the university level.

In 5754 (1993-1994), after graduating high school, Roi decided to study at the pre-military yeshiva program (*mechina*) Bnei David located in the community of Eli [a settlement located in southern Shomron], joining the sixth class to graduate the program. Roi adjusted naturally to the *mechina* and was described by his rabbis as extraordinarily serious at his studies. In Eli, Roi was able to devote his youthful exuberance and his many talents to the study of the profound writings of Rav Avraham Yitzhak Hacohen Kook, writings that served him as a compass as he continued on the path of life. At the same time he also worked hard at developing his physical fitness, he participated regularly in the training sessions for reconnaissance units in the wee hours of Thursday nights, and just before his enlistment in the IDF he intensified his training according to a personal program that he set for himself.

Roi invested great efforts in order to get to where he could make the greatest contribution while in the army. He was not deterred by failure, as when he was not accepted into the pilot's course or into *Sayeret Matkal* (most prestigious of the elite units). Eventually he was placed in the 'Orev' company of the Paratroop Brigade, in the August '94 enlistment group. In 5755 (1995), a decision was made in the IDF to establish a small, elite unit that would specialize in anti-guerilla fighting with the purpose of improving the level of combat in southern Lebanon against the Hizbullah. Roi's team was transferred in its entirety, together with other teams from select units, to a new company: the "Egoz Reconnaissance Unit" and his red beret was exchanged for the brown beret of the Golani Corps. Roi was to spend most of his military service in this unit.

This course of training, that included active service, was not easy, especially for Roi, who had to work harder than others to meet the physical demands of the grueling regimen, but Roi – faithful to the statement that had become his motto – "Tough is good" – overcame all of the physical and emotional difficulties and became an accomplished combat soldier who was especially gifted in navigation. In 5756 (1996) Roi was sent by his unit to an officer's training course, and upon completing it, returned to the Egoz Reconnaissance Unit as a commander of new recruits and later – as a commander of an operations force.

Ever since finishing his studies in Eli, Roi longed for the study hall and did whatever he could to continue studying Torah even during his taxing army service. At that time he participated in establishing a study group of his friends from Ra'anana, a group which met on Friday nights to study Rav Kook's 'Ein Aya' [a commentary on the non-halachic sections of the Talmud]. Over time the group gradually dwindled but Roi persevered in his study and hardly missed a single session. The soldiers under his command remember him studying Torah on various occasions in the field, in a jeep, or in the army camp.

Roi continued to advance within the army and, in parallel, to intensify his Torah study and the depth of his Torah understanding. In 5758 (1998) he served as deputy commander of a company. Afterwards, like many other newly-demobilized soldiers, he traveled at length, and upon his return, was one of the first to join the beit midrash for graduates of the *mechina*, a program which was just being established in Eli. After several months, he returned to active army duty and accepted command of the Egoz training units. As a commanding officer, too, Roi's style was characterized by a unique ability to reconcile qualities that seemed to be conflicting: when he was in charge of young recruits, he knew how to be tough with them in order to harden them and transform them from civilians into combat soldiers, and when he was in charge of seasoned soldiers he knew how to treat them with respect and to motivate them to carry out their assignments willingly, without having to fall back on his formal authority.

During this period, Roi was fighting almost exclusively in southern Lebanon and over the course of the years, accumulated almost six months of active experience in concealed-position ambushes. Though the ambushes were located in the most dangerous areas of southern Lebanon, Roi never once encountered any terrorists in his entire term there. Despite this, he never allowed his senses to dull and he continued to prepare for each ambush with extreme seriousness and with the utmost professionalism.

In 5760 (2000) the Israel Defense Force withdrew from the security zone that it had established in southern Lebanon. In preparation for the withdrawal, Roi asked the commander of Egoz, Hagai Mordechai, for permission to plan and be in charge of an ambush deep in the enemy zone in which the young soldiers-in-training of Egoz would participate, in order to "get a taste" of the fighting in Lebanon. The sudden withdrawal, not at the scheduled date of departure, found the team sent by Roi at the height of activity with Roi himself on high alert in an IDF outpost in Bint Jbeil. Roi witnessed the IDF's panicked escape and he and his team, who were evacuated hastily by helicopter, were apparently the last soldiers to leave the security zone. Roi carried away with him those grim scenes and anticipated that the day would come when Israel would be forced to return to southern Lebanon, under difficult circumstances.

The period after the withdrawal from Lebanon was a hard one for the Egoz unit, whose original *raison d'etre* had been removed. Roi – now in the position of commander of an operations company in the unit – did not give up and together with other officers in Egoz sought to engage the enemy, and looked for a way to make use of the experience that he had accumulated in Lebanon on other fronts. His opportunity came in 5761 (2001) when he was asked to prepare an operations plan to deal with the terrorist bands firing upon IDF forces in the Shechem area. The commander of the regional brigade was very impressed by the young officer and preferred his plan to an alternate plan which had been submitted. During the period that he was active in this zone, he showed great determination and did not hesitate to demand that his commanding officers change operational details that he thought required improvement.

The high point of this activity was an extended ambush operation manned in rotation by two companies of Egoz. Towards the end of Roi's tour of duty in the ambush, just a few hours before being replaced by the second company, a terrorist cell was identified advancing with the intent of placing explosive devices on the road leading to the army camp on Mt. Eyval. Roi showed himself to be extremely coolheaded when he delayed the order to open fire until the terrorists came into very close range. Once that happened, Roi's force opened fire hitting three of the terrorists. As a result of this action, two of the terrorists were killed and the third was wounded; however, Roi refused to be satisfied with what had been achieved and he immediately put another ambush into a concealed position overlooking the terrorists' bodies. As he anticipated, a short while later an ambulance arrived on the scene with terrorists who had came to evacuate the bodies and to place explosive devices in the way of IDF forces. Roi took this band by surprise as well and managed to eliminate three additional terrorists. The Head of Central Command [an IDF major-general] gave Roi a special citation for the successful operation, which had proven that infantry ambushes are effective also in Judea and Samaria. Roi, with characteristic modesty, refrained from telling anyone about the citation which he stashed under his bed.

During that period, Roi met the person who was to become his closest study partner, Rav Eliezer Kashtiel, who was teaching the students who had returned to Eli after their IDF service. When Roi asked for permission to join the group, Rav Kashtiel told him that they were already in the middle of studying a very difficult subject, but Roi answered: "Tough is good", joined, and became the outstanding member of the study group.

In 5762 (2002) Roi met Sarah Sjalin, and within a short time it was very obvious to both of them that they wanted to build a life together. In *Nissan* they were married and established their home in Eli. The family expanded: two children were born – Gilad and Yoav. During that time Roi was sent by the IDF to study for his BA, a respite from active service that allowed him to spend time building his young family. Roi was a devoted husband and an exemplary family man, who invested in his children, often playing and taking walks with them. Many residents of Eli remember clearly the picture of Roi with his baby slung in a carrier or seated in a baby carriage, on the way to the synagogue or just walking on the street.

Roi chose to study industrial engineering and management. Although he had been accepted at the Technion, which is considered more prestigious, he preferred to attend the College at Ariel so that he could continue to live in Eli and spend more time studying Torah. During that time Roi's daily schedule began at five in the morning when he would drive to Rav Kashtiel's house to pick him up and the two would study together in the Kollel in Eli until the late afternoon, almost without a break. Only few people knew how much he was studying at that time. Together with Rav Kashtiel Roi studied many chapters of the more difficult tractates of the Talmud in depth, large parts of 'Hoshen Mishpat' [Jewish monetary law] in the Shulhan Aruch, and books of Jewish philosophy, especially the works of the Maharal of Prague and Rav Kook. In his gemara studies, Roi particularly enjoyed intensive in-depth analysis, identifying the central axis around which an entire issue revolved, and delving into the traditional commentaries, *Rishonim* and *Aharonim*, on the subject. Roi advanced in his understanding and anyone who was in contact with him could not help but notice that – despite all of his attempts to play it down – he was growing stronger in Torah understanding and *yirat shamayim*. Only in the afternoon would he find time for his university studies, which he completed graduating *magna cum laude*. When it became time to write his final thesis together with his friend Benny Kuperman, the two thought that instead of writing about maximizing the economic efficiency of a commercial company, as was the general practice, it would be better to establish a precedent by writing about the improving the efficiency of a charitable organization, which is what they did.

At the end of 5765 (2005) Roi and Sarah moved to the *Yovel* neighborhood in Eli, which was built in the highest hilltop in the region. The move was inspired by their desire to strengthen the Jewish hold on the land there. On that hill the Klein family lived as neighbors of the Kashtiel family, which allowed them to maintain contact even after Roi completed his studies and returned to active military service.

In early 5766 (2006), Roi began his position as deputy commander of Battalion 51 in the Golani Brigade. Despite the difference between this battalion and the Egoz unit, and despite the fact that he was returning from a long leave of absence for studies, Roi took up his new position quickly and successfully. A special 'chemistry' developed between him and the battalion commander, Yaniv Assor, who consulted with him extensively on what was happening in the battalion. Roi used his sense of humor to alleviate some of the tensions that develop because of the Sisyphean nature of army work and created an atmosphere – relaxed socially but uncompromising professionally – that benefited the operation of the battalion. Despite the intensity of his work, Roi did not give up his daily Talmud study and when he fell behind in his timetable, he would use Shabbat to catch up. He loved the rank-and-file soldiers and never "pulled rank" to set himself apart.

The grim security situation of 2006 found Battalion 51 in the heart of the action. After an IDF soldier was kidnapped and abducted to the Gaza Strip, the battalion fought in this area but following the escalation on the northern border, the battalion was called upon to move northward where it very quickly emerged that they had been entrusted with a difficult and dangerous mission, namely, to capture the Hizbullah "capital", Bint Jbeil.

On the first day of Av, just before 5:00 A.M. when the battalion approached the outskirts of the village, Roi sent an advance infantry platoon to seize a certain house. In the course of the attempt, Hizbullah terrorists shot at the platoon commander, Amihai Merhavia and wounded him. Merhavia reported his wounding and continued to advance towards the source of the fire, with the object of outflanking the terrorists and striking at them, but before he managed to reach them, he came upon a wall that prevented any forward movement, and he was mortally wounded by a hand-grenade hurled towards him. Additional soldiers from his platoon were also wounded. No one knew at that point that a large number of terrorists, armed from head to foot, were hiding behind the high wall, only a few dozen meters from the scene. Roi advanced to the yard where Merhavia was hit and under fire, tried to extricate him.

While Roi and his radio operator were trying to remove Merhavia on a stretcher that had been passed to them by Shimon Adega, who was killed afterwards in the battle, Roi suddenly noticed a hand grenade that had landed right near him. It was clear that the grenade's detonation would injure and kill many soldiers who were in the yard behind the wall at the time. There was not enough time to warn them or to run, and it was also impossible to throw the grenade far enough away to minimize the damage. In the split second that he had, Roi threw himself on the grenade and his body absorbed the full impact of the blast. The soldiers who were nearby heard him cry out 'Shema Yisrael'.

Roi was mortally wounded but he remained alive for several minutes longer. In those minutes, he managed to instruct his soldiers to find cover and return fire. To the soldiers who came to evacuate him, he said: "Go to Merhavaia, to Merhavia". A witness from the battle claimed that Roi tried to operate the communications device and report his own death. His soldiers thought that he was no longer alive until Itamar Katz, an officer who was attached to the unit during the fighting, approached him and they were amazed to see Roi lift his arm and give Katz his encoded communications device, to prevent it falling into enemy hands.

Roi was buried in the Mt. Herzl Military Cemetery on his 31st birthday, leaving behind a wife – Sarah, two small sons – Gilad and Yoav, parents – Aharon and Shoshana, and two sisters – Yifat and Noa. The man who had always sought contact with Torah scholars was buried alongside the former IDF Chief Rabbi, Rav Gad Navon zt"l.

Roi's act of heroism amazed many people not only in Israel but also throughout the Jewish world. Without any prior coordination, the rabbis of many congregations mentioned Roi in their sermons on the High Holy Days following the war, as an example of *Kiddush Hashem* that was worthy of tipping the Divine scales of justice in favor of all the Jewish people. In the year after his falling in battle, many commemorative projects were established in the various fields of activity that characterized his life: Torah study, heroism, leadership, education, and more.

In Elul 5767 Roi was posthumously awarded the IDF's Medal of Courage, for the supreme heroism that he had displayed in his last battle.

May his memory be blessed.

In memory of the eight heroes of the Battle of Bint Jbeil

1 Av 5766 (July 26th, 2006)

Major Roi Klein

Captain Alexander Schwartzman

Lieutenant Amihai Merhavya

First Sergeant Idan Cohen

First Sergeant Ohad Klausner

First Sergeant Shimon Dahan

Sergeant Shimon Adega

Sergeant Assaf Namer